The Dual Disorders
Recovery Book

The Dual Disorders Recovery Book

A Twelve Step program
for those of us with addiction and
an emotional or psychiatric illness

What we used to be like,
what happened, and
what we are like now

Hazelden Publishing

Hazelden Publishing
hazelden.org/bookstore
800-328-9000

Book design by Timothy Quinn McIndoo

Library of Congress Cataloging in Publication Data
The Dual Disorders Recovery Book: A Twelve Step program for those of us with addiction and an emotional or psychiatric illness.
       p.   cm.
Adaptation of: The Twelve Steps.
Hazelden Publishing—T.p. verso.
ISBN: 0-89486-849-8
1. Dual diagnosis—Patients—Rehabilitation. 2. Twelve Step programs.
I. Hazelden Educational Materials. II. Twelve Steps.
RC564.68.D83 1993   92-34149
616.86'0651—dc20   CIP

Editor's note
The characters in this book are composites of many individuals. Any similarity to any one person is purely coincidental.

The Twelve Steps are reprinted and adapted with permission of Alcoholics Anonymous World Services, Inc. Permission to reprint and adapt the Twelve Steps does not mean that AA has reviewed or approved the contents of this publication, nor that AA agrees with the views expressed herein. AA is a program of recovery from alcoholism only—use of the Twelve Steps in connection with programs and activities that are patterned after AA, but that address other problems, does not imply otherwise.

Alcoholics Anonymous has generously given permission to use quotations from *Alcoholics Anonymous* [also called "The Big Book"] (New York: AA World Services, Inc., 1976).

CONTENTS

Foreword, *Cardwell C. Nuckols, PH.D.*, vii

How It Works

1 Michael's Story, *Michael J.*, 3
2 Hope and Healing: A Comprehensive Approach to Dual Disorders, *A. Scott Winter, M.D.*, 27
3 The Twelve Steps and Dual Disorders, *Abraham J. Twerski, M.D.*, 44
4 We Agnostics, *Genna L.*, 55
5 Recovery and Relapse, *Kate S.*, 63
6 Abstinence and Sobriety, *Kate S.*, 69
7 Telling Others, *Jody N.*, 73
8 The Stigma of Mental Illness, *Jody N.*, 89
9 To the Family, *Paula Phillips, M.A., A.T.R.* 102

Personal Stories

Alan's Story, 111...Daile's Story, 118...Donna's Story, 123...Eric's Story, 131...Genna's Story, 135...Jay's Story, 144...Jody's Story, 152...Judy's Story, 170...Kate's Story, 183...Kathy's Story, 190...Raven's Story, 199...Roberta's Story, 202...Scott's Story, 211...Willie's Story, 213

Dual Recovery Anonymous

Dual Recovery Anonymous: A Blueprint,
Timothy H., 221
Dual Recovery Anonymous: Meeting Format, 232

Resources, 239
The Twelve Steps of Alcoholics Anonymous, 241

FOREWORD

Cardwell C. Nuckols, PH.D.

THE SUBJECT MATTER of this book is one of great importance to me, personally and professionally: I suffer from the dual disorder of addiction and posttraumatic stress disorder (PTSD).

Twenty years ago, I spent time in jail for several marijuana misdemeanors. Being in jail in a southern state for a drug crime during the early seventies was truly unfortunate. The jailers considered addicts more devious and criminal than murderers. For a young man raised in a rural, upper-middle-class environment, my experiences were overwhelming. During my nine-month stay, I saw rapes, a knifing, and other crimes that horrified me. For years after my release, I had recurrent nightmares. I would not talk to anyone about these experiences, and I was extremely guarded and angry. This undiagnosed posttraumatic stress disorder severely hampered my ability to enjoy my early recovery from alcohol and drugs. Working the Twelve Steps was important and helpful, but serenity was elusive. Only after professional mental health counseling was I freed from the shackles of PTSD. Now I am freely enjoying my recovery for myself and with my family. Psychology and self-help have been powerful allies in my life.

Many studies and statistics have attempted to explain why individuals with alcoholism and other addictions succeed in recovering and why others fail. The studies and the statistics may be difficult to understand, but they document the lives of many who struggle with the disorders of alcoholism and other drug addiction.

In many Alcoholics Anonymous meetings over the years, I have heard that one-third of those who join AA get better almost immediately. They seem to be able to recover simply by working the Twelve Step program. Another third struggle, often for years, before recovery becomes theirs. These people may have difficulties for many reasons, but ultimately they grasp AA's program. Another third rarely seem to recover, although they may sincerely strive to work an honest program of recovery. Despite their grave and painful attempts, recovery eludes them.

"The Big Book" of Alcoholics Anonymous describes these individuals in the following passage: "Those who do not recover are people who cannot or will not completely give themselves to this simple program, usually men and women who are constitutionally incapable of being honest with themselves. There are such unfortunates. They are not at fault; they seem to have been born that way. They are naturally incapable of grasping and developing a manner of living which demands rigorous honesty. Their chances are less than average. There are those, too, who suffer from grave emotional and mental disorders, but many of them do recover if they have the capacity to be honest."* This one-third of

---

Alcoholics Anonymous [also called "The Big Book"] (New York: AA World Services, Inc., 1976), 58. All quotations from *Alcoholics Anonymous* are reprinted with permission of AA World Services, Inc.

individuals suffering from alcoholism who repeatedly fail seem to have a character disorder or other significant psychiatric problems. They have dual disorders, and they seem to be incapable of grasping this program of recovery.

I often wonder about this failure. Are these individuals *unable* or *unwilling* to recover? In my experience, I've found that they are in no way unwilling. Over the years I have witnessed the desperate struggles of individuals with alcohol and drug problems who have gone from psychiatric treatment to alcohol and drug detox centers and then back again to mental health treatment programs. I have seen their willingness to try several kinds of treatment and have empathized with their pain, frustration, and failure. Typically they are not unwilling; rather, they are often unable to work the program because of psychiatric problems that coexist with the alcoholism or other drug addiction.

Bill W., founder of AA, suffered from depression so severe as to make him bedridden at times. His moods could sway from despair to extreme optimism. During the mid-1940s, his depression deepened; he was seldom free of despairing moods and saw psychiatrists on a regular basis. But throughout this time, Bill W. was able to find lasting and successful recovery from alcoholism in the program that he and Dr. Bob inspired.

From the earliest history of Alcoholics Anonymous, a relationship has existed between psychiatry, psychology, and AA. The AA term "spiritual conversion"—that is, the point where grandiosity and defiance give way to an inner sense of harmony and connectedness—first appeared in a letter Bill W. received from the famous psychoanalyst Carl Jung. Discussing an individual with alcoholism who, in spite of the greatest effort, could not seem to recover, Jung credited the person's eventual recovery to a conversion of the spiritual kind. This letter first documented the potential for a successful marriage between medicine, psychiatry, and what would eventually become the self-help movement.

Don't be discouraged if you suffer from alcoholism or drug addiction and another disorder such as anxiety, depression, personality disorder, or schizophrenia. Many people with dual disorders have been able to work a Twelve Step program that has greatly assisted their recovery. Others have found lasting and serene recovery in AA with the help of counselors, psychiatrists, and, sometimes, medications.

I am fortunate to work with individuals suffering from alcoholism and other addictions. Where else could one see the marvelous and dramatic transformations of early recovery? These great changes seem little short of miraculous. For eighteen years, practicing my profession has been a true labor of love. For the past twelve years, working with others who have dual disorders has brought me great challenge and hope. Those with dual disorders need not fail!

I remember Lenny, a young schizophrenic who was addicted to alcohol, marijuana, and heroin. He had endured countless unsuccessful treatments. Over and over, he was either detoxed and put back on the street or else sent to a psychiatric crisis-stabilization unit for large doses of medication. Never was he treated for both problems at the same time.

Individuals with dual disorders must be given integrated chemical dependency and psychiatric treatment, treatment with integrity, and tremendous understanding. Although sometimes difficult to love, Lenny needed love more than most. Ultimately he found the family he so desperately needed—the members of an AA clubhouse. His sponsor helped him stay clean and encouraged him to keep taking his medication.

Lenny has multiple chronic illnesses—alcoholism and other drug disorders plus schizophrenia. He will be alcoholic, drug-addicted, and schizophrenic for life. These problems do not go away. To say that Lenny is in recovery is to say that his schizophrenia is stable, or that he has "compensated." He remains free of alcohol and drugs one day at a time. Lenny's attendance at self-help meetings and his psychiatric treatment, including medication, are a winning combination. He now has periods of serenity. Isn't that the goal of self-help and treatment? Moments when heaven descends?

When relationships with people are established, and when control over the alcohol, drugs, and psychiatric disorders is given up, help becomes possible. As in the case of Lenny and so many like us, it is a simple, concrete Twelve Step program that brought meaning to our lives.

I remember Margaret, a twenty-nine-year-old incest survivor who had endured an extremely traumatic childhood. She was addicted to cocaine and alcohol and had an eating disorder. Margaret also suffered from borderline personality disorder—her identity was so severely disturbed, she did not know who she was. She suffered from depression and had attempted suicide on several occasions; her wrists were proof of these attempts. Her adult life had been a long series of bad relationships. No matter how she tried, Margaret could not stay out of harmful relationships. She would go to a self-help meeting and immediately fall in love with the unhealthiest individual there. Typically, sobriety for Margaret and her partner would last between two hours and two weeks.

What Margaret needed so badly was a protective parent— her mother was an alcoholic and her father had abandoned her. She had never known anyone she could trust and who could be counted on to help her, at least not until she began working with two special people—a therapist and a sponsor. Her therapist, who was trustworthy, helped her discover herself. Her sponsor, a recovering alcoholic who had once attempted suicide, was available to Margaret and kept her away from relationships that had destroyed her recovery in the past. Her sponsor became the parent that Margaret had never had. Here again is the power of connection and the power of mutual help. Ours is truly a program of hope and opportunity.

I recently reflected on a term that I have used over the years: *home group*. The dictionary says *home* is "a place of origin," where one is "at ease or in harmony with the surroundings"—on familiar ground. *Group* means "two or more figures forming a complete unit" or "a number of individuals assembled together having some unifying relationship." The home group is a powerful part of the prescription for the individual with a dual disorder.

Addictions and psychiatric or emotional disorders (anxiety, depression, personality disorder, and schizophrenia) have many things in common. Both are predictable and treatable, and both have signs and documentable progressions. Therapists, doctors, and medications may be very important for some who suffer from dual disorders, but these methods work best when the individual is connected to a harmonious surrounding, that special place that really is a home for recovery—the home group.

Most people with alcohol and addiction problems come into Twelve Step programs as loners, rebels, and pessimists. As loners, we have difficulty fitting in. As rebels, we never want to look bad in front of a group. As pessimists, we believe recovery can never happen to us. The individual with a psychiatric or emotional disorder has great reason to be pessimistic. We have frequently been mistreated by those we trusted. We can feel lonely because often we just don't seem to fit in. But when medical science is integrated with the program discussed and witnessed in this book, the miracle of recovery becomes more possible than ever.

I believe two things to be true: The Twelve Step program saved my life, and psychotherapy and prescribed medication cannot replace the need for a group, which can become a haven or a home. But together, medicine, medical research, therapy, and self-help offer great hope to those of us who have tried and failed on the separate paths of self-help or treatment.

Please open your heart and your mind to the following chapters. Read carefully the struggles of those men and women whose lives have been remarkably changed through their willingness to work the Twelve Step program and to seek professional help.

May God bless you and your recovery.

How It Works

There are those, too, who suffer from
grave emotional and mental disorders,
but many of them do recover
if they have the capacity to be honest.
ALCOHOLICS ANONYMOUS

1
MICHAEL'S STORY

Michael J.

What It Was Like: The Perfect Boy

I WAS THE boy most likely to succeed. I was the perfect kid in a perfect family, but my perfect family and I were, in reality, something other than perfect.

My mother had her first psychotic break—paranoid schizophrenia—when I was two, and she was in and out of mental hospitals for the next three decades. This was before antipsychotic drugs, and she was subjected to electric shock treatment, water (torture) treatment, and other enlightened therapies. She could not give me love and instead alternately terrorized and abandoned me. My scant memories of her include her nonpsychotic state, when she compulsively watched my every move to make certain I cleaned up after myself.

Recently, I recognized that perhaps even more significant than my mother's insanity was the simple fact that she did not love me or really want me in the first place. A political activist before her insanity, she ran for a seat on the city council while she was pregnant with me. To her credit, she was the first woman to be elected to that position in my hometown. But I was an interruption, a bother. When I was a baby and toddler, I was frequently left alone. I'm told that one time, the family dog and I wandered downtown and were gone for some time. Finally, someone who recognized me brought me home and lectured my mother—who evidently had not known I was missing.

From the time I was two, my mother's insanity dominated our home. She was seldom physically violent, but the atmosphere of anger and violence surrounded our home like a cloud, and sometimes I huddled in my bed and went into space in my head rather than hear the screaming—my parents screaming at one another, my sisters screaming at one another, or my mother or my oldest sister screaming at me. And sometimes there was physical violence. My sister remembers, but I don't, my mother breaking a wooden spoon over me as a teenager, beating me because I wouldn't bring my dirty gym socks home to be washed.

My mother's illness was a family secret, never to be discussed.

My father, on the other hand, loved me. Unfortunately, his love was controlling and sometimes violent. I grew up under his thumb—the feeling was more like growing up in a pressure cooker. I had no alternative but to be perfect (and to be a doctor like him). When I was in grammar school, he would give me a dollar for every A that I got but take away two dollars for any B. I would not have dared come home with a C. He lectured, cajoled, manipulated, and finally *ordered* me to skip eighth grade, in order to better position me for the scholarship I would eventually win. He browbeat me into skipping my fourth year of college so that I would move more quickly into the successful career in medicine he had planned for me. Ultimately, I was supposed to move back to my hometown and take over his practice after he retired.

Dad was a beloved town doctor, but he was sadistic toward his kids. He rubbed my lips with hot chili peppers to see my reaction. My reaction was fear and tears, of course. He hit me frequently, and if I protested in pain, he would say it was his way of showing me affection, proudly adding that he never hit me in anger.

When I was perhaps thirteen, he shot me with a shotgun in a hunting accident. I screamed, stung physically and emotionally. Some shotgun pellets had penetrated my hand, and there was a trickle of blood. Evidently my father thought I was lying or being a "whiner" again. He didn't come to check out my wound but yelled at me from a distance to go back to the car and wait for him to finish hunting the hill. He was angry with me for being in the way of his shot at the quail. He always wanted to toughen me up.

There was always something wrong with me; I was a *lazy, stupid kid*, never good enough.

While my mother modeled paranoia, my father taught it to me directly: The world was full of Nazis, he told me. Nearly everyone was a fascist underneath, and we'd better watch out. I had to learn to protect myself and be safe. The way to be safe was to learn to shoot a shotgun and be a doctor.

But strangely enough, my father also showed me the most love and kindness I was to receive as a young child. I have a picture of him holding my hand and helping me learn to swim when I was four years old.

The most loving care I received was when I was very sick. One of the few good memories I have of my childhood is of when I had polio. I was in the polio ward at a hospital with other boys. We played together and were treated with wonderful tenderness and tolerance by the nurses there. I recovered quickly and completely. I learned that being sick and unhealthy was my only hope of being loved and cared for. This was training me to later take on the role of the victim— to be the smoker, the psychotic, the identified "sick" person.

But in my youth I was "perfect." The perfect son was, in fact, perfectly dissociated—that is, I had no sense of my own feelings, no sense of myself. My life was a performance, the object being to survive, without my even understanding that I was performing. I lived in various states of fear without realizing it. I hid from my mother and my violent oldest sister, and I would not make any mistake my father or siblings might catch. I steeled myself physically and emotionally. For me, everything was always okay. Whatever it was, I could handle it. I shoved the self-hatred and terror so far down I had no idea it existed.

I achieved. I was high school student body president and a nearly straight-A student (I was distraught when I received one B in high school), an all-around athlete, and winner of the scholarship my father had wanted me to get. I went on to a major university, became engaged to a beautiful young woman, and was accepted to a major medical school after just three years at the university.

But living out my father's script for my life slowly began to take its toll. In college I tried to go wild, without actually doing so. I partied, smoked marijuana, sometimes drank myself into a stupor, took courses in writing and literature instead of biology. But my compulsive achievement held sway, and my grade averages were good enough to get me into medical school.

While in medical school, I became torn. The academic pressures of medical school had combined with the stress of the late 1960s—the social upheaval and anger against the war in Vietnam. I began to boil with rage at an unjust world. I had dreams about shooting older men—presidents and generals involved in Vietnam, my symbol of injustice in the world. I broke up with my fiancée in rebellion against being a settled, stable person. I couldn't stand up to my father—I didn't even feel anger toward him. I believed he knew best and that I *should* do what he wanted. It was for my own good, after all. But I had the growing feeling that something was wrong: I was not living my own life.

In my second year of medical school, at age twenty-two, after months of torment and one semi-serious attempt at suicide by way of sleeping pills, I dropped out to join a hippie group and travel around the world. After taking too many drugs in Kathmandu, Nepal, I broke into hallucinating psychosis. Self-hatred and fear burst out of me and into the air, becoming *they* who wanted to consume me and turn me into a zombie, a walking dead man. *They* were a giant conspiracy led by the Hindu goddess Kali and the innumerable demons, spirits, and human beings who followed her. Kali, the fiery goddess of destruction, wore human skulls as a necklace and danced on the bodies of the people she destroyed. I had to be constantly alert, or the voices in the air would invade me and take over my soul. My days and nights were a constant struggle against these demons: I couldn't move, I couldn't speak, without the action somehow becoming part of the battle for my soul.

The struggle was mostly telepathic: I thought most people could hear my thoughts and I could hear theirs. At night, I lay awake fighting, struggling, screaming at them in my mind to fend them off.

But I was alone, and *they* were everywhere, and everyone I knew seemed to know about it but for some reason either didn't care or were allies of Kali and her demons.

[7]

I could not talk about this conspiracy to destroy me; it was another secret I had to keep. While in Kathmandu, I engaged the inner demons more and the outer world less. My travel companions saw me disintegrating and could do nothing for me other than suggest I go back to the States. I became less and less coherent as I spoke out loud to the demons in the special language of the conspiracy. (Today, when I walk by a homeless person on the streets engaged in a vocal struggle with invisible adversaries, I feel a strange mixture of sadness, fear, and gratitude.)

I lived in a room in a building owned by a Tibetan family who lived in the rooms next to me. My Tibetan landlord—a wonderful man—saw that I was in trouble and decided that I must be possessed. At his own expense, he hired a Tibetan monk to try to exorcise my demons. The monk and I sat in my room and chanted all day. I had some hope, but when the monk left, the demons remained.

I tried to alleviate the terror with all the drugs I could get my hands on. I took methamphetamine (speed) to wake up and feel better, and I took barbiturates to sleep. I smoked hashish to smooth out the speed. I took opium, LSD, and cocaine when I could. Dying of drugs and disease in Kathmandu was the fate of many young people in those years, and I was almost one of them. People said that I looked like a walking skull. I called my father, and he bailed me out with a plane ticket back to the States.

I didn't realize the voices were delusions until one day, months later in California, I heard my cousin and her husband-to-be taping a cassette to send as a voice-letter to friends. I *knew* they were talking about me, using the special Tibetan-English-Nepalese lingo I *knew* people used behind my back. I later sneaked into the room, listened to the tape, and discovered they were talking about nothing more serious than the weather. I decided something was wrong with me and that maybe I needed treatment.

A county psychiatrist who visited my hometown once a week said I was a chemically induced schizophrenic and gave me Stelazine, an antipsychotic similar to Thorazine. I visited him a few times, then stopped. I think he was a kind man but had little experience with treating someone he probably thought of as a "burned-out hippie." I was hallucinating and probably should have been in intensive treatment. Our sessions were awkward; I became uncomfortable enough not to continue seeing him—but I did continue taking the Stelazine.

The next few years were nightmarish as I struggled with the voices and received no other treatment—with the exception of my father yelling at me, telling me I had ruined my stupid life and if only I had listened to him. . . . I lived in isolation, on guard against the demons. As the voices subsided, I grew more miserable than ever. I wrote poems and called my cousin to read them to her and lament my life—and, bless her, she listened to me. I bought a handgun and periodically played with it, loaded, sometimes holding it to my temple. I used food and drugs such as marijuana, heroin, and barbiturates to try to dull the pain. I had gained about sixty-five pounds on junk food. Eating canned soup and bologna sandwiches, I developed a nutritional disorder, a nerve paralysis of my face that took weeks of vitamins to cure.

I was functional enough to hold easy jobs, and eventually I improved enough to get a job as an insurance agent. In a new environment with new hope, I got clean from most drugs. I had even stopped the Stelazine, but I still used marijuana and Valium. Over the course of three years, I thought I was cured and had a new life.

My new life and career were to be short-lived, however. Under the stress of a conflict with a friend who was also my boss, I had a full relapse. The demons pursued me again. Sometimes I'd get up in the middle of the night and drive a hundred miles to try to lose them.

At least I had enough sense to seek help, and soon I was in a county-run day treatment center as a permanently disabled chronic paranoid schizophrenic. The doctor told me I would never work again and a normal life was out of the question. The staff helped me apply for and get Social Security Disability (SSD). Friends had left in tears after watching me disintegrate; I had no idea why they were crying.

The doctor prescribed three times the dosage of Stelazine I had taken before. The dosage made me stiff, blurred my vision, and felt like an anchor on my brain, but at least it quieted the voices. Beyond the medication, I believe it was the gentle kindness of a nurse, Louise, and the safety of the day-treatment environment that saved my life. Louise sat on the couch, told me to lie on my back, and put my head in her lap. She stroked my forehead, soothing my burning mind. She talked gently to me—I haven't the slightest memory of what she said, but I heard that I was okay. I believe this helped more than any group therapy or individual analysis.

Once again the voices subsided, this time after only several months. As I settled down, I detoxed down to a low dosage of Stelazine and was discharged from the clinic.

Coming out of this second and final psychotic break, I began to pour myself into political activism. It was a woman named Linda who brought me to this work. Linda liked me and wanted me to work on a political campaign. Soon I was managing the campaign, writing pamphlets and campaign literature, and appearing on radio and television. I came out of the psychosis like a shooting star. I had nothing but time on my hands, my brains to use, and new interests (Linda and a political cause) in life. I became a hero, because Linda believed I could be a hero. I was riding high. (I was "over" my illness except that I still took low doses of Stelazine, and I detoxed entirely several years later.) I was in love and achieving remarkable things. I was a success story once again.

But finding love and purpose only in external and female form, I would come back down the path of depression and addiction. Though a friend to this day, Linda moved on. I turned to other political work and other short-term relationships.

Eventually I found myself working fourteen hours a day or more in a political cult that demanded my life and in return gave me regular, severe criticism about my numerous shortcomings. The criticism sessions were supposed to strengthen me for the struggle against the fascists. They wanted to toughen me up. This was familiar abuse, of course. It felt just like home to me, and my new compatriots even remarked that I was like a fish in the right water. I continued the drop toward oblivion.

If a woman showed interest in me, we'd be instantly deep into what would turn out to be a short-lived relationship. I didn't know it, but I was afraid that any serious relationship would consume and destroy me in a repetition of my earliest intimate relationships with my parents. So I pretended at intimacy, and when things got too close and I couldn't pretend anymore, I found a way out.

My terror of intimacy showed up as a need to control and manipulate. If I was in control and was never honest about my needs and wants, I wasn't vulnerable—or so went the illusion. My relationships with women were characterized by the feeling of responsibility for their lives, guilt if anything went wrong, longing for them to take care of me and fix me, and the need to analyze their problems and heal them. I had many relationships, and while they were not abusive, they were short and often stormy, ending in meaningless arguments. I was deathly afraid of being close, while at the same time, I desperately wanted to be loved and fixed.

My relationships with men were characterized by fear, distrust, and distance, with the exception of a few friends who evidently did not remind me of my father. I had many male "buddies," and I related well in sports and games, but if ever a man became an authority figure to me, I hated him and wanted out as fast as possible. This is what had happened with my friend and boss in the insurance business.

In all relationships was the specter of psychosis. To be close meant that I might be subjected to stress, and stress meant that I might lose my mind again.

For me, life became a string of fixes. The political work itself had become a fix: Perhaps I could make up for being an awful person by saving the world from all its injustice and cruelty. When not working, I was eating, smoking dope, or losing myself in the television set. When I could, I used prescription drugs or narcotics.

After several years of trying to fix my way around life, I was feeling the advent of an early death. I was at least sixty pounds overweight and going up the scale. I was on two high-blood-pressure medications and having occasional heart arrhythmias; smoking four packs of cigarettes a day; using whatever drugs were available; and working fourteen hours most days. I was deeply unhappy and lonely working in the midst of a political community all day long. I was a basket case looking for a basket.

After a particularly miserable and lonely holiday season— I had to work constantly for the political group and developed an arrhythmia that was frightening to me and difficult for the doctors to stop—I dropped out of the cult and retreated to my parents' home. I was there alone while they were on an extended retirement vacation. I shot morphine for a couple of months but then ran out of it and money.

What Happened: Reaching Bottom

At that time, I thought of myself as a crazy, fatally flawed person, a monster and a failure who couldn't even make up for being a miserable person by doing good political work. I now understand things about my life that I couldn't have known earlier. For one thing, my "paranoid schizophrenia" was a misdiagnosis. As I understand it now, I suffered from PTSD (posttraumatic stress disorder). Like a war veteran, I had been subjected to prolonged trauma and not allowed to work through the feelings resulting from the trauma. The trauma started when I was two, with my mother's psychosis; it continued throughout my entire childhood with the emotional violence and cruelty in our home; and I was allowed neither to show "bad" feelings nor discuss any of them. There was no shoulder to cry on, no safe place. As a young adult away from home, I blew up and fell apart, and my psychosis resembled paranoid schizophrenia. My paranoid delusions weren't the fantastic invention of a biochemical imbalance. They were the externalized expression of the inner world I had learned as a child. The world was an evil place that wanted to destroy me, and I was a stupid monster that the world would rightly destroy if it found me out. The demons had exploded out of my core into the world. Drugs such as LSD helped catalyze this explosion, but I had been a time bomb waiting to blow up.

Similarly, my chronic and sometimes suicidal depression wasn't a genetic flaw of some sort. Depression didn't "run in the men in our family," as a male cousin put it. It may, however, have run in our family system. I felt awful almost all the time, because my life had been awful. In my childhood, I had taken too many doses of unprocessed abandonment, fear, and cruelty; consequently my adult life was composed largely of insanity, dysfunction, and addiction. There may have been biochemical changes in my brain relating to depression, but if so, I believe the changes were the results, not the cause, of long-term emotional trauma. I remember being eight years old, hearing my mother and father scream at each other, watching my older sisters fight like cats and dogs, hiding in fear, knowing that at some point all the rage would come my way. I remember thinking, "Why is anyone alive? This is no fun. I don't want to be alive." And that was perhaps my average day. My depression was a sort of chronic, deep despair: It was my legitimate response to a miserable life experience and to decades of repressed anger, fear, and sadness about that experience.

Sitting in my parents' house, though, dropping out for the second time from what I thought was my life's work, I knew none of this. Instead, I fixated on a single refrain: I have no permanent home, no job or prospects for work, no car, no money, no friends, no significant relationships. I had taken strike three: There was nothing left. My life was over.

With the morphine gone, I was sick with body aches, stomach pains, headaches, and a nose that wouldn't stop running. I wanted to disappear and reverse my birth, wipe out the fact that I had ever existed, but I was unwilling to actually take my own life. I don't know exactly why I was unwilling. I can say that throughout my life, even in the worst times, there was a part of me that longed for life, longed to reach out and connect with something real. I had written poems and called my cousin instead of using the gun. Instead of driving over a cliff, I had allowed the nurse, Louise, to reach me. Somehow, I just wasn't done yet.

I still had my typewriter. I started writing again. I wrote a poem about wishing I'd had a mother. Writing and redrafting that poem, one day I started to cry—the first flow of tears in my adult life. I started to touch my grief for my lost life. Somewhere at the bottom of that grief, deep inside, there was hope and a growing spark of will to live.

I now believe this was the beginning of my opening to myself and to something greater than myself. I was broken enough to begin dropping my walls to my own grief and to a power that had been resting at the bottom of my being.

At the time, however, I wasn't able to recognize the source of my strength. As I started feeling better, all I knew was that I wanted another shot at life. As a good child of my family, I put away those silly, unproductive feelings of grief. After all, I had my brains and I could get a loan. I moved out of my parents' home to live with the same generous cousin and dear friend who had helped me in the past. I bought a computer, created flyers, and called myself a computer consultant.

Over the course of three years, I landed increasingly better jobs, did good work, and started making a decent living. I even found myself in a significant relationship. She bought a home, and I moved to live with her.

After burning out on nearly a decade of trying to save the world, I started instead to look for answers about my own life. I was living among people who practiced one form or another of spirituality, and I found myself drawn toward "inner work" and spiritual exploration. I couldn't believe in an anthropomorphic, Judeo-Christian God, but I was drawn toward other practices: I went to the woods with Robert Bly and the men's movement; I studied the works of Joseph Campbell; I danced the Spiral Dance with those who honored the Goddess and the earth; I took inner journeys in shaman circles, bought a drum, and collected small, precious objects. I gained something special from each of these practices as I joined others reaching for the truth, reaching toward the mystery, and I began to perceive that there was more to the universe than the material world. I no longer used drugs and had given up cigarettes, but the food addiction was getting much worse: I was up to perhaps 300 pounds. I had stopped weighing myself when I reached 292 pounds.

Something was missing. I couldn't have said it myself and would have argued with anyone who had, but despite my new spiritual practice, I was still avoiding my life. My inner work was not yet genuine; I was still seeking the answers in the experiences, ideas, and feelings of others.

What was missing was the practice of the Twelve Steps. At the urging of a friend, I started going to Overeaters Anonymous (OA) meetings. At first I had great resistance to what I thought was a Christian fundamentalist cult. I needed "translation" services in the form of a good sponsor, and I found one.

After a few months, the OA program began to put substance, community, and action into my nascent spirituality. I began to transform as I worked the Steps. The Steps gave me a way to begin letting go of the heavy control I tried to practice in my daily life. I began to live more honestly, do service, examine my own actions and behavior, and account for myself. I began to clean up my life.

Working the Ninth Step was a profound experience for me. In making amends, I found I was not the person I thought I was. Nearly everyone I went to with amends was glad to hear from me, thought of me warmly, and didn't want to talk about my owing them something. They listened to me chatter about how awful I had been, told me I wasn't so bad, and asked why I hadn't written lately. I made new friends of old friends, discovering that maybe I wasn't such a monster after all. One of the most delightful of these connections was with my fiancée of twenty years past. I had carried so much guilt and longing, feeling I had wronged her badly and she could only hate me. I called her and broke down crying in apology. She told me that she was glad to hear from me and that she remembered me with love and warmth. To her, our breakup was the result of two people coming together who were too young to know what they were doing.

I became abstinent from my most difficult addiction, food, and began to lose weight. My blood pressure dropped to normal, and I ran twenty miles a week. I felt alive as I had never been. I was becoming healthy and active, engaging in activities—skiing, for example—that I couldn't have dreamed of doing at three hundred pounds. Now that I was no longer so self-destructive, my relationships with others became healthier as well: more honest, open, and supportive.

Life was joyous and rose-colored as I lost one hundred ten pounds and regained breath and vigor. But it wasn't rosy for long. Perhaps by now I could have seen the patterns of my roller-coaster life, but it seems I was never ready for the trip down. With my newfound stability and safety in the world, a year of abstinence, Step work, and therapy, a lifetime of suppressed feelings began to rise like an ocean tide. Everything I had worked so hard to keep down was coming up.

When the feelings first came, I thought that god had entered my chest, because I couldn't otherwise name what was going on inside. Crying frequently, I shared seriously in meetings that I was having moving spiritual experiences about twice a week.

I began to realize that I was experiencing emotions and that I didn't recognize them because I couldn't remember having had any. I had been living in a prolonged, dissociated state of fear and, for my survival, had become quite good at faking a range of emotions. My act must have been good because it sure fooled me, but now I had to practice recognizing and naming emotions.

New recognitions came up over the course of months. It was hard enough to realize that I'd been living in an unconscious state for forty years, but then I realized, with a shock that lasted weeks, that I didn't remember any part of my childhood that included being with my family, and many other parts of my childhood were missing as well. I just hadn't thought about it before; denial is an amazing phenomenon. I discovered I had multiple inner children—not one dissociated state, but different ego states or combinations of states into which I would dissociate, depending on the type of situation I needed to survive. It dawned on me that I did not have the slightest idea who I was, who all these inner children really were, all these parts of me, all these tiny voic-

es that could be demons, giants, and monsters when life was too much.

It was as if I had checked myself at the door instead of my coat, and I had been missing for forty years while the coat had dinner. As my situation became clear, I slowly became an open, raw wound.

So began the hardest work I have ever participated in: healing my life. There was a lifetime of repressed grief, pain, anger, and fear to remember and experience, a lifetime of fear-based behavior to change, a paranoid and fragmented inner world to transform. It's the work of the heart on the heart of all my addictions, dysfunctions, and emotional problems. I think it's the work that needs god the most.

What is god? I don't know, but I can talk about my experience. There are times in meditation I touch a tiny part of a vast, compassionate spaciousness—a presence that seems to be more the loving space for a presence than a presence itself. It seems deep within me yet extends far beyond. At these times I know that my existence is a gift and that my life has a purpose. I believe I have touched the source of my healing and my humanity, and it is something deathless and infinitely kind. Now there are many times in my everyday life, not just in meditation, when I feel this presence. Meditation and prayer have helped me a great deal.

During this period, I needed my god a great deal, because when I proceeded into my unexplored inner world, there were times I wanted to die; times I fell to the floor paralyzed with anxiety; times I thought I was going crazy again; times I couldn't walk down a street without the sight of a mother and child filling me with unbearable sadness and loss or the sight of a couple filling me with jealousy and pain. I resented the life my god had given me, but I trusted that there was

healing and maybe even some purpose to it all. I left my Twelve Step-oriented therapist for one specializing in healing from deep abuse.

For a brief period, I could feel the voices on the edges of my perception, and I would need to take Stelazine again for a few days. Each new memory or recognition sent me reeling for days or weeks. Though close relationships were overwhelmingly painful, I continually sought relationships to relieve the pain, and I learned something about loving relationships and toxic ones as well. With each divorced part of myself, with each inner child, there was a battle to go through, a reconciliation to be found, a new—and this time nurturing—relationship to be established.

I could not be around my parents without getting physically sick. Ultimately, I had to confront my father and stand up to his continuing abuse, his berating, demeaning attitude toward me. Then he died unexpectedly in his sleep while visiting my sister, ten days after the significant confrontation. I had massive new guilt and torment to work through with the belief that I had killed my father.

My life, no longer a string of fixes, had become a thunderstorm of pain, anxiety, and desperation. At times I lost my sense of community, lost friends, lost loving relationships, lost my food abstinence, and lost my connection with my god. I had found a new Twelve Step home in SIA (Survivors of Incest Anonymous). Survivors *felt like* my peers, even though I could remember no specific sexual abuse. I sometimes shared in these meetings that I had one good day for every ten days of feeling miserable, and I started smoking again.

There were times I felt broken to my core, when I prayed to god to let me die, or screamed at god for giving me this

life and for answering my prayers for healing only with more devastating memories and feelings.

Luckily, the Twelve Steps, the community of other recovering addicts and abuse survivors, a wonderful therapist, a few dear friends, and the connection with my god were harbors against the storm. In the worst times, I continued the work, motivated by the memory of hope, the memory of love, the memory of the will to recover, and just plain obstinacy. My screams at my god were mixed with prayers for hope and the willingness to try. I continued meditation, therapy, and sharing with others even when I could not attend meetings, and I tried to live by the principles of the Steps. I continued my technical writing work, though for some months my production was less than good—I am grateful to have had an understanding boss at the time. I found considerable help in the work of recovery writers and speakers, and help in those who taught me Buddhist meditation and to find the healing in the center of pain and grief.

Slowly the process of healing continued even when I felt I was sliding into darkness. The emotional crisis that had seemed only to deepen over nearly three years slowly began to lift.

What It's Like Now: Recovering My Life

It's common for abuse survivors to go through an extended crisis such as the one I experienced. As the memories and recognitions flood up, our perceptions about our lives are turned upside down and inside out.

Yet there are other kinds of understanding that also carry meaning for me. The crisis lifting was like slowly coming out of a firestorm. I think about Kali. Two decades ago, I knew her only as the horrific, multiarmed goddess

of destruction whose goal was to consume my soul. Later I began to psychologize her as the combined vision of my mother and older sisters attacking me. I was young, and they seemed to be giants. But Kali, the Hindu goddess, has meanings more subtle than destruction; she is another face of god. Her fire is the energy of life and death: It burns away the flesh of illusion and leaves the bones of reality. To burn in the fire may be painful beyond words, but maybe it is a blessing to have the opportunity to lose the illusions, lose the deceptions and acts and addictions and the baggage that keep us from ourselves, from others, and from a genuine experience of life. The false has to die, as everything has to die, to make way for the truth and for new life. There is a mystery and awe to reality—a beauty, even a painful beauty and a painful joy—in the experience of life and the world. I *need* to take part in life, the mystery, the reality. To do so, I needed to go through the fire. In order to fully live, I need to face my life, and this has often been extremely painful and not under my control—but worth it.

It is over a year since my father's death and several months since I stopped experiencing my life as an ongoing crisis. The uphill climb seems to have become less steep for now, though I don't doubt I'll find some cliffs and canyons on the trail.

I am fifteen years out of day treatment. It's been twelve years since I've had to use Stelazine for any period longer than a few days and seven years since I've used illegal or legal drugs in any significant way. Though I've had my bouts with food addiction, I've had four years of freedom from continuous, oblivious bingeing, and I am sixty pounds below my top weight of about three hundred. I no longer work myself into the ground, and I refrain from leaping headlong

into relationships. I jog for a half hour two or three times a week, and the days I don't jog, I take long walks with my dog, a wolf-hybrid who happens to be the sweetest, most wonderful animal in the world.

I still contend with the ghosts of the past but not so desperately. I pray for help and willingness in letting go of cigarettes; this struggle brings me face-to-face with more ghosts. Smoking points out how a large part of me wants to remain a victim: It's a sure way to be unhealthy, but it doesn't get me loved and cared for.

Cigarettes also affirm the role of despair in my life; they're a form of suicide. They dampen the feelings, fog over the fear, create a buffer between others and myself, between me and the *awful* world, the source of potential disappointment and despair. Letting go of cigarettes is breaking a physical addiction and psychological habit, but it is also part of the process of letting go—asking for and allowing the lifting— of habitual despair about myself and the world.

I work the Steps, and time will tell whether the cigarette addiction will be lifted. I no longer want to affirm the despair, and I want to stop being a victim.

I am single, still have fear about intimacy, can be very insecure, and have difficulty reaching out; sometimes I am painfully lonely. But I do reach out, I have friends, and I make new ones. After some well-paid years as a self-employed computer professional, I took a leap to buy my own home. Somehow I feel that my ultimate work is not writing computer manuals, and I often wonder what my life's work really is and how I can get to it. But work is another major issue for me, given my father's frequent curse that if I did not become a doctor, I would be a failure.

At forty-four, I'm an emotional teenager wondering what

I'm going to be when I grow up and whether I'm going to have a significant relationship.

I am off the roller coaster, I hope, and onto a lifelong road toward healing, on which I've taken the first few steps. For me, the healing is found in the course of the thousands of thoughts and events of each day.

Each time the fear comes or I start to beat myself up or steel myself against my feelings, if I can breathe and soften my body and send a little kindness into my chest, there is healing. This softening and opening help keep me from returning to addiction or from being a "dry drunk"—clean of substances but compulsive and driven in other areas of life.

Each time I let go of trying to control and simply do my best at what I need to do, there is healing. When I write to get to the heart of a problem, when I am honest rather than masked with those to whom I am vulnerable, when I listen openly to others and share in a recovery setting, when I can help someone else, there is healing. When I can recognize that I have dissociated and be gentle with myself and allow the return to my body in a time and way I cannot control, there is healing.

When I let go of little wrongs, the healing is there. And when I refuse to be abused and get angry with someone who's tromping on me, it's there as well. The healing is in my abstinence, in my exercise, in taking care of myself and my inner children, in playing and singing when the mood hits, in getting a massage or taking a hot bath when it's cold. It's in relaxing and being lazy when I need to relax and be lazy, and in not beating myself up about it. It's in observing my dysfunctional ways and making amends when I have done harm, in accepting and forgiving myself for my dysfunction while doing what I can to change, in exploring my

lost memories and the roots of my condition so that I needn't compulsively relive the past.

The healing is in asking a new friend to take a walk with my puppy and me, and it's in the warm bond between me and my puppy. It's in letting myself feel love for the puppy and in letting myself feel the pain of knowing how short her life may be. It's in taking risks and in honoring the part of me that is not yet ready to take a particular risk.

When I meditate to make space in my heart, there's healing, and it's there when I ask my god for guidance or to remove my self-hatred and fear.

The healing is in trying, and it's in giving in to the pain, anger, grief, and sadness to find the hope that lies underneath.

The evidence of my healing is the slow transformation of my world from a place filled only with hatred, fear, cruelty, death and war, abuse, greed, poverty, and injustice into a place that has love, joy, kindness, and compassion in the midst of, despite, and beyond the tragedies. And perhaps my healing contributes a little to the end of abuse and injustice in the world.

There is a different quality to my life these days, a growing quality of acceptance, clarity, aliveness, and growth. I am lonely, but I am not desperate to get "fixed," and without the desperation, I become less lonely. I have fears of intimacy, but I am willing to face the fears and trust myself more in moving through them. I may not know what I'm going to be when I grow up, but I know my life has a meaning that is seeking fulfillment. Even my pain is my own pain—the price of being alive and mortal—and not the suffering of someone trying to avoid himself and everyone else. Today, I was feeling lonely and sad after visiting a friend I knew I would not

see again for a while, but I thought, *At least this is me: This is my sadness, my loneliness, as well as my happiness at the thought of having friends I care about enough to miss. And I am no longer burying it all, skipping my own life.* And there was a softness to the feelings, not the hardness of someone steeling himself against himself.

I'm not free of all my compulsions and dysfunctions, but many are lifted, many behaviors are changed for the better, and most important, I am no longer driven by addictions or crazy behavior. I am liked and valued by friends for who I am, not for being a good act. In my journey, I have gained insight and compassion and I have helped others on the path.

Now there are times I know a quiet, soft happiness. I may be driving down the street or sitting at my computer. I put my attention inside my chest and feel a warmth spread softly through me, bringing a smile to my face. I think about the Promises, about comprehending serenity and knowing peace.

2
HOPE AND HEALING:
A COMPREHENSIVE APPROACH
TO DUAL DISORDERS

A. Scott Winter, M.D.

ACCORDING TO THE dictionary, the word *diagnosis* means "the act of identifying a disease from its signs and symptoms." When you have a nagging cough, your doctor examines you to find out what's causing the problem. Is it bacteria, a virus, or an allergy? To get the right treatment, you need the right diagnosis.

Dual disorders—sometimes referred to as dual diagnoses—present a double challenge to mental health caregivers (including chemical dependency counselors, clinical social workers, psychiatrists, psychologists—the entire treatment team). When two serious illnesses exist in one person at the same time, each can complicate the other. Teasing these tangled threads apart to make an accurate diagnosis—and more important, to provide effective treatment—becomes much more difficult.

In the not-too-distant past, caregivers often assumed that any emotional problems seen in people with chemical dependency were merely symptoms arising from the substance abuse. Typically, when people who abused drugs or alcohol

also suffered from a disorder such as depression, they were told, "The addiction is your basic problem. If you stop drinking and drugging, your depressive symptoms will vanish." Their doctors would hospitalize them, dry them out, perhaps refer them to a Twelve Step program—and then scratch their heads, wondering why these people would relapse. Or they might have been treated only for their psychiatric condition while their chemical dependency was all but ignored.

Meanwhile, the suffering of people with dual disorders continued. Even if they stayed sober, they still wrestled with depression, anxiety, or other emotional turmoil. Often their symptoms were so serious that they began abusing substances again, hoping for relief, and the cycle would begin anew. As if things weren't bad enough, they also had to wrestle with the social stigma of mental illness. Through ignorance or insensitivity, other people looked on them as weak-willed or morally bankrupt, rather than as affected by not one but two devastating illnesses. They were seen as failures. The truth was, treatment had failed *them*.

Fortunately there's been a lot of progress over the years in the treatment of chemical dependency. The introduction of the Twelve Step philosophy in the 1930s was the first major advance. In 1952 the American Medical Association recognized alcoholism as a disease, a concept that the public has gradually come to accept. Federal anti-drug efforts, combined with increased social pressure and health awareness, have done much to reduce the abuse of drugs and alcohol.

We have also greatly increased our understanding of dual disorders. Today we in the mental health field are less likely to get hung up on the question "Which comes first, the chicken [chemical dependency] or the egg [various other psychiatric conditions]?" Instead, we see that people can indeed experience two or more psychiatric problems—drug or

alcohol abuse and an emotional disturbance—*at the same time.* What's more, we know that the chemical dependency does not always appear first. Sometimes, for example, a person with agoraphobia (essentially the fear of leaving the house) becomes dependent on the anxiety medications prescribed for the condition. Estimates are that three out of ten people with substance abuse problems have an underlying mood or anxiety disorder as well. Each of the diagnoses requires its own form of treatment. Most important, we now realize that spiritual healing, in addition to physical healing, is essential for complete recovery.

Risks and Realities

People with dependency problems are more likely to develop other psychiatric conditions than the general population. Conversely, people with psychiatric problems are at much higher risk of becoming substance abusers. According to the National Institute of Mental Health, if you suffer from a phobia, for example, you are nearly two and a half times more likely to become chemically dependent. For people with bipolar disorder (manic-depressive illness), the risk is more than *fourteen times* as great as that of the average person, and more than *fifteen times* as great for people with antisocial personality disorder. The following chart spells out the risks (compared to those of the general population) associated with some of the major psychiatric illnesses.

If you have a diagnosis of . . .	*Your risk of substance abuse is:*
Phobia	2.4 times as great
Obsessive-compulsive disorder	3.4 times as great
Major depression	4.1 times as great

If you have a diagnosis of . . .	*Your risk of substance abuse is:*
Panic disorder	4.3 times as great
Schizophrenia	10.1 times as great
Manic-depressive disorder	14.5 times as great
Antisocial personality disorder	15.5 times as great

Drugs and alcohol alter mood. That's why people use them. Those with a psychiatric disorder—depression, for example—may drink or take drugs in an attempt to alleviate their emotional pain. This is known as self-medication. The chemicals they use may provide some relief but do nothing to correct the basic emotional problem. As soon as the drugs wear off, there it is again: that dark, hopeless cloud of depression. They pour themselves another shot or light up another joint, and the cycle begins again. Over time they become totally dependent on substances to regulate their moods. In this scenario, chemical dependency *masks* the psychiatric illness.

On the other hand, someone may be using drugs that poison the body and brain. Over time the ability to think and function is lost. The person feels sad, hopeless, and guilty. Sleep and appetite are disrupted. On the surface, these appear to be the classic symptoms of depression. Deeper down, they are the toxic results of substance abuse. In this case, chemical dependency *mimics* the psychiatric illness.

You can see why dual disorders pose such a challenge. As a psychiatrist, it's my job to identify your true condition so that we can work together to help you get better. As long as you are abusing substances, I won't know if the emotional disorder causes you to crave drugs or whether the drugs produce the emotional disorder. That's why the key to successful re-

covery from dual disorders lies in first stopping all use of drugs or alcohol. Only then can we get a clear picture of your problem. At that point we can attack dual disorders on two fronts by treating both the chemical dependency and the psychiatric illness. Ordinarily it is best to treat the chemical dependency first, but, as I'll explain shortly, there are exceptions to this rule.

Psychiatric Disorders: An Overview

At this point it will be helpful if you know more about some of the specific psychiatric disorders that often exist alongside a chemical dependency. The list is long, so I'll focus only on those that crop up most often.

Mood disorders: Half of all the cases of dual disorders I handle involve a mood disorder of some kind. Mood disorders appear in two basic forms: depressive disorders and bipolar (or manic-depressive) disorders.

The most severe of the depressive disorders is major depression. This crippling condition causes a period of low mood accompanied by sadness, guilt, hopelessness, decreased energy, loss of enjoyment in life, and suicidal feelings. Depression can last for many weeks or even months. Eventually depression may lift by itself, but given proper treatment, a person's mood usually returns to normal within a shorter time. Another depressive disorder is dysthymia, a less intense but longer-lasting form of the illness.

Bipolar disorder occurs less frequently than major depression, but it is in some ways more severe. The main feature of this illness is the intense mood swings from depression to abnormal elation, or mania. (Technically, people can have

bipolar disorder even if they experience only the manic phase.) During manic periods, people usually feel either euphoric (physically or emotionally high) or extremely agitated. They may not sleep for days on end. They often talk a mile a minute, but their thoughts don't seem to connect. They may have grandiose ideas about themselves or their work. Frequently they behave in inappropriate ways—launching new businesses, spending all their money, having a string of sexual affairs, and so on.

The other mood disorders are variations on depression and bipolar disorder. The differences involve the severity of symptoms, length of time they persist, or how rapidly and how often the person swings between the depressed and the manic phases.

Depression is widespread; over a given six-month period, nearly ten million Americans will suffer bouts of depression. This troubling condition affects all aspects of a person's life: the body, the mind, and the emotions. Depression is far more serious than a temporary case of "the blues." People with depression can't simply "snap out of it." They need treatment, love, and understanding.

Substance abuse, especially alcohol abuse, makes the mood disorder worse. In my experience, fully half of the people whose alcoholism involves depression will find their moods are markedly—if not completely—improved after three weeks of sobriety. If the depression persists, there are many effective treatment strategies we can try. Approximately 80 percent of people who seek help for depression get better.

Anxiety disorders: Anxiety, panic, phobia, obsessive-compulsive disorder, and posttraumatic stress disorder are all part of the spectrum we call anxiety disorders. A certain amount of

anxiety is normal, even helpful, in our daily lives. In anxiety disorders, however, the body seems to have lost the ability to control its anxious feelings. The brain in turn may cause the person to act in exaggerated ways in a desperate effort to relieve the tension.

An anxiety disorder involves a powerful and unpleasant mental tension with no apparent cause. Symptoms include shaking, sweating, dry mouth, pounding heart, and rapid breathing. People with anxiety often worry that something bad is about to happen to themselves or their loved ones. They are impatient, irritable, and easily distracted. Anxiety is an even more common disorder among the general population than depression.

Panic disorders affect more than a million people in this country. A panic attack is unpredictable. It produces intense, overwhelming terror for no apparent reason. When panic strikes, many victims think they are having a heart attack.

A phobia is an intense feeling of terror or dread that some people experience when they confront certain objects, situations, or activities. Phobias are strong enough to interfere with jobs, family life, and relationships. Among the common forms are social phobia (fear of situations involving other people), simple phobia (fear of snakes, for example), and agoraphobia (fear of being alone in a public place with no escape route, such as a moving bus).

Obsessive-compulsive disorder affects more than two million Americans. Obsessions are repeated, intrusive, unwanted thoughts, such as thoughts about violence against a loved one. Compulsions are ritual-like behaviors that the person can no longer control. Typical compulsions include furious housecleaning, repeating a behavior (such as washing hands), or endlessly checking locks on doors. Both obsessions and

compulsions are ways people try to cope with severe anxiety. No matter how many times the thought or the behavior is repeated, however, the anxiety persists.

People with anxiety disorders often turn to alcohol and other depressant drugs to try to calm themselves down. The truth is, these chemicals can produce the opposite effect. Anxiety is almost always worse after the booze wears off than if it had never been used. Thus substance abuse only worsens the impact of anxiety disorders on a person's social, personal, and professional life.

Dissociative disorders: Sometimes people suddenly feel they are not "connected" to the real world—in other words, they are dissociated from it. If these moments of dissociation occur often enough and are serious enough, they can become a true disorder. Dissociative disorders disturb or alter one's identity, memory, or consciousness. They can cause periods of "lost time" in which people suddenly realize they can't remember what happened during the past few minutes. At one time we assumed these disorders were relatively rare. In recent years, however, we've learned that perhaps as many as five out of every hundred people experience some kind of dissociation in their lives—memory disturbance, amnesia, or identity confusion.

One of the most well known of these conditions is post-traumatic stress disorder, or PTSD. This disorder (officially classified as an anxiety disorder but sharing many of the traits of other dissociative disorders) affects people who have survived severe physical or mental trauma. People with PTSD suffer from nightmares or flashbacks, emotional numbness, anxiety, depression, insomnia, and poor memory. They are easily startled and have trouble concentrating.

An extreme and strange form of dissociation is multiple personality disorder, or MPD. MPD wasn't recognized as an official psychiatric diagnosis until 1980, which meant that for years the many people who experienced multiple personalities weren't treated at all for this disabling condition. MPD is a direct result of severe childhood abuse and occurs in women three times as often as in men. People with MPD have two or more distinct personalities, each with its own relatively consistent pattern of perceiving, relating to, and thinking about the self and the environment. Also, at some point, at least two of these personalities alternate in taking full control of the person's behavior.

Many people who experience dissociative symptoms use drugs or alcohol, hoping to relieve the terror of feeling out of control. One study found that 46 percent of people with MPD abuse drugs and 42 percent abuse alcohol. As with most dual diagnoses, it can be hard to distinguish the effects of chemical dependency from the symptoms of MPD. For example, blackouts or periods of lost time are common features of both dissociation and substance abuse. Some of the MPD patients I've treated have one or more alternate personalities, or "alters," who are chemically dependent and some alters who never touch drugs or who are sickened by the slightest sip of alcohol. Also, many people with alcoholism have a "drinking personality" that comes out when they are under the influence of liquor. This personality may be angry or violent or loving. When the alcohol wears off, the personality disappears. People with MPD may also display sudden changes of personality. If such people abuse chemicals, the doctor who is unaware that MPD is present will likely assume that these behaviors are triggered simply by use of drugs. Clearly, in such cases, treatment for alcoholism alone will not relieve the

problem. Fortunately, the growing awareness of MPD means more caregivers are likely to spot the warning signs and offer effective therapies for both conditions.

Personality disorders: There are a number of personality disorders that involve deep-rooted, inflexible, and harmful ways of thinking and relating to other people. All of us have personality traits that may give us trouble at times. A personality disorder, however, is a persistent pattern that is serious enough to cause suffering both to the individual and to other people, and which makes it hard for the person to function in a meaningful or productive way.

Some personality disorders are more often associated with substance abuse than others. As the figures I mentioned earlier show, people with *antisocial personality disorder* are at tremendous risk for using mood-altering drugs and alcohol. Such people are frequently troubled, tense, and unable to tolerate boredom. They drink or use drugs to relieve tension. By definition, these people are antisocial; that means, in part, they have little respect for laws, including laws against drug use. Under the influence of alcohol or drugs, people with an antisocial personality often unleash their anger and become abusive and violent.

People with *borderline personality disorder* are also prone to flare-ups of anger and violence, especially when substance abuse is involved. Borderline personality describes those who have a lot of uncertainty about many basic life issues such as self-image, personal values, friendships, and sexual orientation. They tend to see everything in terms of black and white. They can become very hostile when they don't get their way. They may regard another person as their best friend one moment and as their most hated enemy the next.

These people typically abuse stimulants to bring on feelings of pleasure, or they may abuse depressants to relieve distress. People with borderline personalities walk a thin emotional line: use of drugs and alcohol can push them over the edge.

Another common disorder is the *dependent personality disorder*. This is different from codependency, which describes a type of relationship rather than an actual psychiatric diagnosis. People with a dependent personality disorder have trouble making everyday decisions. They need constant reassurance, prompting, and advice from others. Fearing rejection, they will go to extreme—even unhealthy—lengths to please others. Often they find themselves in a codependent relationship with someone who is chemically dependent or who has a psychiatric illness. Many times people with a dependent personality begin using drugs or alcohol in an effort to appear supportive or less threatening to their mates. In time they risk becoming addicted themselves.

Schizophrenia is a debilitating illness that affects perhaps one person in a hundred in this country. There are different types of the disorder, but generally symptoms include bizarre behavior, nonsensical speech, strange or disjointed thinking, and an impaired ability to experience or express emotions. People with schizophrenia often have delusions about who they are—they may believe, for example, that they are Abraham Lincoln. Or they may believe they have special powers, such as the ability to communicate with aliens. They often experience hallucinations, such as hearing voices that others around them cannot hear.

The firestorm of schizophrenia makes its victims more susceptible to the use of mood-altering drugs, especially

depressants. Schizophrenia robs people of their grip on reality; they are unable to think clearly about the consequences of their actions, including drug use. Another problem is that schizophrenia usually requires lifelong medical treatment. People with the disorder often resent having to take medication and may forget or refuse to do so. Without medication they invariably suffer relapse, and their symptoms flare up again. In that stage, they are more likely to turn to illicit drugs or alcohol for relief. The sad thing is, they won't find it there.

Two other problems are often associated with chemical dependency: *eating disorders* and *sexual compulsions*. Indeed, food and sex sometimes serve as "intoxicants," in the sense that they can profoundly alter mood, and the pleasure they offer can be so intense that some people develop insatiable appetites for them. There are many similarities between substance abuse and compulsive use of sex or food: denial, loss of control, continued use despite growing problems associated with the habit, secrecy, shame, and a strong tendency to relapse after treatment. One difference, however, is that people with sexual or food compulsions seldom develop physical tolerance—that is, the need for higher and higher doses of these intoxicants to achieve the same effects.

The two main eating disorders are anorexia and bulimia. (Compulsive overeating is usually considered a physical or metabolic disorder rather than a psychiatric one.) Anorexia is self-starvation, arising from a desperate desire to be as thin as possible. Bulimia involves overeating followed by self-induced vomiting or other extreme steps to get rid of the food. Eating disorders symbolize people's desire to gain control of their lives; food intake may be the only thing over which they feel in control.

Many people with eating disorders—more than 90 percent of whom are women—use stimulant drugs to control their appetite. They may become dependent on caffeine or diet pills and often progress to more powerful, illegal amphetamines or to cocaine. Many abuse laxatives and diuretics. People with bulimia frequently begin their binges by drinking an entire six-pack of beer or a bottle of wine. With their inhibitions and judgment gone, they proceed to gorge themselves until they vomit or fall asleep.

For people with sexual compulsions, sex loses its function as a way to express tender feelings. Instead, it becomes a "drug" used compulsively to relieve anxiety or to avoid facing other problems. In most cases, sex addiction arises in people who were sexually abused as children. This suggests that, for them, sexual craving is an expression of their desire for the nurturing they didn't get as children.

Predictably, the use of drugs or alcohol by people with this disorder is like a lighted match tossed into a room full of dynamite. Stimulant drugs, marijuana, and liquor often remove whatever inhibitions people might have. The most notorious drug in this category is cocaine, especially crack, which produces an orgasmic rush within seconds after it is inhaled. Many sex addicts report that without drugs, they could have kept their sexual desires on the level of private fantasies. Stimulants are especially dangerous as promoters of promiscuity because people can become addicted to the high they get when they combine drugs with sex.

The Sailboat of Recovery

For the person who suffers from a psychiatric illness, the journey through life is hard. For one who also struggles

with addiction, it's harder still. Envision the process of recovery as a boat with four sails. Each sail represents a different aspect of the process: biological, psychological, environmental, and spiritual. All of these sails must be hoisted and trimmed so that the boat can move swiftly over the rough seas ahead.

The biological sail represents the need to restore the body to its normal level of functioning. Years of substance abuse turn the body into a toxic waste dump. Yet, given a chance, the body has remarkably sophisticated ways of removing these poisons. Abstinence, proper diet, and exercise can restore physical health in relatively short order.

The psychological sail represents treatment aimed at straightening out tangled thinking and correcting harmful behavior. There are many ways to achieve this; therapy with an individual counselor and group therapy are but two examples.

The environmental sail means treating the dual disorders in a broader context. Whatever the circumstances, treatment must take into account the fact that we all live with, and among, other people. Making adjustments to improve our environment means improving our chances at getting better.

Finally, the spiritual sail offers the opportunity for healing that is rooted deep within the heart and soul. It is the sail that keeps the boat of recovery moving forward even if all the other sails are tattered and torn.

Diagnosis and Treatment: A Brighter Picture

Most of the people with dual disorders who come to me for help usually do so because of problems directly related to their addiction and not because of their underlying psychiatric

problem. They are brought in by worried friends or family members, or they have been ordered by their bosses or a judge to get treatment. Even if they haven't been caught in the act of using drugs or alcohol, their lives are obviously falling apart as a consequence. They may look like hell: puffy faces, red eyes lined with pain, unkempt or unclean appearance. Or they may be completely unable to function on the job or at home. In most cases, these people don't come of their own accord. A crisis must usually take place—medical emergencies, threats of divorce, lost jobs, or jail terms—before they will put themselves in the hands of a caregiver.

The first task is usually to address the chemical dependency. The exception is when people are brought in because of a psychiatric emergency, such as a severe manic episode, suicide attempt, or a complete break with reality, as in schizophrenic psychosis. In such cases the immediate crisis must be dealt with first. The manic mood or the schizophrenia must be brought under control; treatment for substance abuse has to take a backseat. One thing the mental health field has become more aware of in recent years is the need to address each person's individual situation. A rigid approach won't work; the goal is to first take care of the problem that most threatens the overall welfare of the person (or in some cases, the family).

Often, though, treatment begins by addressing the addiction. The first priority—the biological sail—is detoxification, which is the use of medications, diet, rest, fluids, and good old-fashioned tender loving care to bring the body back to normal. Detox from the highly addictive drugs, such as alcohol, barbiturates, heroin, and cocaine, is a challenge because of their severe withdrawal symptoms. Recently, though, it's been discovered that a medication called clonidine blocks the

symptoms of narcotic withdrawal. Bromocriptine is useful in assisting withdrawal from cocaine. Other medications show similar promise in helping smooth the pathway to a drug-free body.

Only after detox is complete will I be able to get a clear look at the person in my care. This process—trimming the psychological sail—can take two or three weeks. During this period I will spend hours in conversation with my patients (and, ideally, with as many members of their families as possible) trying to find out what makes them tick. I will pore over the results of psychological testing looking for clues that show me how they feel about themselves and their lives.

During this time I also look at the person's entire world. Problems in the marriage or on the job may need to be addressed. Perhaps someone else living in the patient's home continues to abuse alcohol. Adjusting the environmental sail prepares the patient to deal with problems he or she may face after leaving the safe, sheltered world of the treatment center.

And, as soon as possible, I raise the spiritual sail: I encourage people with dual disorders to attend meetings of the Twelve Step group most suited to their needs (Alcoholics Anonymous, Narcotics Anonymous, Overeaters Anonymous, and so on). Most treatment programs now recognize the tremendous value of the Twelve Step approach. Many hospitals even offer Twelve Step programs within their own walls.

The genius of the AA founders was that they devised a program whose principles and philosophy can benefit anyone seeking a new and better life. Over the years, such programs have helped thousands of chemically dependent people overcome their addictions. The Twelve Step program

offers the strength, support, and understanding that only comes from others who have walked that road before. In meetings people feel free to express and explore their feelings. They gain perspective by hearing from others who are struggling with similar feelings and issues. By attending meetings, people with dual disorders can get sober and stay that way. They are then better equipped to deal with the psychiatric disorders that may have contributed to their chemical dependency in the first place.

Some people tend to see Twelve Step programs and the medical-psychiatric approach as incompatible. While that might have been true in the past, it is certainly less true today. Most self-help programs recognize the need for appropriate treatment in the hands of a professional. Likewise, most of us in the mental health field now realize that ongoing, self-directed spiritual healing is essential. As a psychiatrist, I see the Twelve Step philosophy as one of my greatest allies in helping people recover from dual disorders.

Mental health caregivers today are more alert to the special needs of people with dual disorders. We offer effective team treatment aimed at resolving not just one but two or more complex and serious illnesses. Whether your journey of recovery has just begun, or whether you are continuing your journey, know that there is hope. Healing lies ahead.

3

THE TWELVE STEPS
AND DUAL DISORDERS

Abraham J. Twerski, M.D.

JUST AS RECOVERY from a physical illness requires that we make changes in the way our body works, recovery from a dual disorder—an addiction and an emotional or psychiatric illness—requires that we make changes in how we think, feel, act, and react. Some of these changes may require specific, nonaddictive medications; some may require psychotherapy; and some may require reworking our character.

During the past half-century, the Twelve Steps of the Alcoholics Anonymous and Narcotics Anonymous programs, among others, have proved effective in bringing about the character changes necessary for recovery from addiction.

Although we usually associate the Twelve Steps with addiction, they may also help people who have never been addicted; the Steps are guidelines to a way of living that can benefit everyone. And while they can be lifesaving for the addict, they can also be a valuable adjunct to recovery from various emotional diseases.

But Twelve Step programs may not be as effective when there's a coexisting emotional or psychiatric disease. This

shouldn't come as a surprise, because the Twelve Steps primarily address the disease of addiction. Just as they are not expected to treat pneumonia or diabetes, neither can the Steps be expected to fully treat coexisting emotional disorders.

The combination of an emotional condition and addiction calls for a careful evaluation of symptoms, because some of the symptoms that we assume to be due to the addiction—e.g., anxiety, lethargy, mood changes—can actually be due to the other conditions. Once we can identify the coexisting diseases and begin proper treatment for the psychiatric illness, we can then apply the Twelve Steps to recovery much more effectively.

Sometimes we may use alcohol or addictive drugs (prescribed or illegal) in an effort to gain relief from anxiety, panic, depression, or compulsions. Here are three scenarios that could precipitate such feelings: (1) Standing in the checkout line at the supermarket, we are suddenly overtaken by an intense feeling of impending doom. We experience tightness in the chest, heart palpitations, and shortness of breath. (This could even occur in the protective calm of our living room or as we sit quietly in church or drive along an uncongested highway.) (2) We find ourselves abruptly thrust into a severe depression, feeling so listless and lethargic that we can't get out of bed, or we feel so agitated, dejected, and despairing that we think of suicide. (3) We find ourselves obsessed by strange thoughts or driven to perform rituals that appear to be senseless, but which we cannot resist doing.

Some of us found that alcohol or drugs temporarily relieved our distress. But when the effect of the chemical had worn off, the symptoms recurred, and we returned to using the chemicals, usually in increasing amounts, eventually resulting in addiction.

When addiction and another emotional condition coexist, it's not that important to know which came first; what is important is that both conditions receive the appropriate attention. We need to become (and remain) stable with our psychiatric condition and abstinent from our addiction. This is where the Twelve Steps can help.

STEP ONE: *We admitted we were powerless over alcohol and other drugs—that our lives had become unmanageable.**

Many of us fight such an admission tooth and nail. We try various methods to control our use of addictive chemicals without outside help, but nothing seems to work. For many, it may take a near-disaster or even a total one to make us realize that we have lost the battle with chemicals. We try repeatedly to gain control of our lives, but we are much like the driver of a car in which the steering mechanism has failed—frantically turning the steering wheel won't change the direction of the car.

When we finally realize that we are out of control and stop our drinking or using, we may expect things to fall neatly into place. But even in an uncomplicated case of chemical dependency, the consequences of years of abuse don't evaporate in a matter of weeks or months. A period of abstinence and a gradual return to rational thinking and responsible behavior eventually eliminate many of the emotional and behavioral problems of the active addiction.

---

*Adapted from Step One of Alcoholics Anonymous, which reads: "We admitted we were powerless over alcohol—that our lives had become unmanageable." The complete Twelve Steps of AA appear on page 241.

Those of us who have a dual disorder, however, may find that even after long periods of abstinence, we are still subject to emotional and behavioral symptoms, such as severe mood swings, episodes of anxiety or panic, obsessive thoughts, or compulsive actions. The dual disorder may seem like a double whammy: We are not in control of our addiction, nor can we control some of our emotions. Acknowledging that our emotional symptoms are beyond our control can help us understand that our addiction is a disease that is also beyond our control. This realization can help us accept our powerlessness over alcohol and drugs.

Being powerless over the emotional symptoms of a dual disorder may require that we turn to a source outside ourselves for help. We generally don't perceive our inability to control depression and anxiety, for example, as a moral weakness, nor do we consider it humiliating to ask for help from a competent professional. When we turn to an outside source for help with an emotional illness of any kind, we are taking the second of the Twelve Steps.

STEP TWO: *Came to believe that a Power greater than ourselves could restore us to sanity.*

If we understand addiction to be a disease and accept that treating it requires help outside ourselves, it may be easier to see that we need outside help with our dual psychiatric disease.

Some diseases, such as the common cold, run their course and improve without treatment. But other conditions require external help. For example, the symptoms of recurrent anxiety, depression, or compulsions can be thought of as a kind of insanity that may require professional treatment and

specific medications, both of which are, in fact, sources of power greater than our own.

It's humbling to have a disease that requires us to seek help from an outside source. (Some people with excessive pride and arrogance have been known to refuse help even for a heart attack!) But asking for help for any condition that is beyond our control shouldn't be considered demeaning. Two cornerstones of spirituality are that we realize our humanity and accept the fact that we must all depend on others.

The idea of *spirituality* is vital to recovery, and it may be good to say a few words about it here.

Human beings differ from animals in many ways. While animals grow primarily in body (bigger and stronger) and in physical functioning, people grow in character development as well. Character includes not only intelligence but also the ways in which we think, feel, and behave. These, in turn, are influenced by abilities that are unique to humans and that make up the human *spirit*.

Human beings have the unique ability to learn from the past; to think about the purpose of existence; to think about and implement self-improvement; to reflect on the long-term consequences of our actions; to delay gratification; and to distinguish right from wrong and act accordingly.

When we exercise these abilities, we implement our spirit; we are then *spiritual,* and our spirituality influences the way we think, feel, and behave.

We grow in character when our thoughts, feelings, and behavior are influenced by valuable lessons from the past—not only from our own mistakes but from historical mistakes as well. We grow in character when we reflect on whether we are already as good as we can be or whether there are some things we can do to make ourselves into better human beings.

Thinking about our goals and purposes in life encourages us to improve ourselves, and this enhances character growth.

Some of our behavior may have been destructive because we acted without thinking about the long-term effects of our actions or because we were unable to delay gratifying our desires. We may have done things because we had an urge to do them, without considering whether they were right or wrong.

Character growth begins with the awareness that we all start out imperfect. Just as we need teachers to increase our knowledge, we need outside help to achieve character growth. When we take Steps One and Two, we plant the seeds of this growth. We recognize that some aspects of our lives are beyond our control and that they may require outside help to bring them under control.

To gain control, abstinence is critical. As long as we use addictive substances, which affect the way we think and feel, we can't see this clearly. We may think things are okay when they're not. Mood-altering chemicals change our perception of reality, and we lose our normal clarity, or "sanity." A dual disorder distorts reality two ways: through the addiction and through the emotional illness.

Some of us may resist Step Two. Although we recognize that we need help from a power outside ourselves, we may assume that the word *power* implies God. Some of us may have difficulty or feel uncomfortable with the idea of God. While some of us do believe in God, many of us have grown up with an adoration of modern science, and we dismiss anything that cannot be demonstrated and proved. Some of us have been brought up with religion but have lost faith in God. The injustices we have seen in the world may seem too great to allow belief in a just God. Some of us have been disillusioned by those who represented religion, and now we

consider religion hypocritical. When we hear that recovery requires believing in a Power greater than ourselves, we back off, thinking that if recovery requires believing in God, then it's beyond our means.

While some of us equate a Higher Power with the traditional concept of God and are perfectly comfortable with it, this is not essential. To recover, we need only accept a Power greater than ourselves, whatever it may be. As one recovering person aptly put it, "When I came to realize what a mess my life was in, I fired the person who was running it." If we fire ourselves as managers, someone or something else must be assigned the job.

To summarize: When we have a dual disorder, we need help from sources outside ourselves, and each condition may require a different type of help.

Since our lives have become unmanageable because of the dual disorder, we take the Third Step.

STEP THREE: *Made a decision to turn our will and our lives over to the care of God* as we understood Him.

At first glance, we may think that we must make a commitment to religion, because the Steps now refer to "God." But the phrase "as we understood Him" allows us a broad choice of what we wish to think of as God.

Consider first the idea of turning our lives over. Submitting our lives to a Power greater than ourselves is not that unusual. We do it when we accept treatment for an illness, trusting that the doctor's knowledge and care will make us well. We do it when we undergo surgery, turning our lives over even more completely. For the psychiatric part of a dual disorder, we are likely to accept treatment (including prescriptions)

from a competent professional, in which case we really are turning our lives over to his or her care. When we turn our lives over to a Higher Power for recovery from our dual disorders, we simply expand our openness to help.

While turning our lives over to others' care is not unfamiliar, the idea of turning over our will does appear to be a new idea; psychiatrists or counselors generally don't ask us to turn our will over to them. Yet turning our will over to a Higher Power isn't really so unusual. As children, we may have wanted things that were not good for us, perhaps candy before dinner or sharp-edged toys whose potential for harm we didn't understand. Our parents, who were then a "power greater than ourselves," told us that these were not healthy choices. Similarly, a doctor may tell a patient with stomach trouble, "You can eat anything you want—and here is a list of things you can want." In other words, sometimes we want things that are detrimental to our well-being. Therefore, we ask for help from a Higher Power, saying, "I want   , but help me to learn what is best for me."

Our addiction affected our will, and we may not be able to see that what we desire is harmful to us. As we recover, we learn to will healthier things, and we turn to our Higher Power to help us correct the distorted will that has kept our addiction going.

To learn where, how, and why we have made unhealthy choices, we take Step Four.

STEP FOUR: *Made a searching and fearless moral inventory of ourselves.*

We know that we are driven by powerful instincts: self-survival, security, prestige, sex. They may be expressed in ways that contribute to health and growth or in ways that harm ourselves and others. Taking inventory means that we take stock of what we've done and review our assets and liabilities. Then we analyze, as best we can, why we did certain things and what the consequences were. This process helps us identify our healthy and unhealthy actions. Just as a business's inventory shows which products generate a profit and which result in losses, a moral inventory helps us to see our character's "profits and losses."

Focusing on our assets and liabilities enhances our character growth, but our efforts may be derailed if we blame others for all our adverse experiences. If we are preoccupied with the wrongs that others have done, we do nothing to help improve ourselves. Only when we identify our own mistakes can we make changes that will help us grow in character.

For example, perhaps we reacted with anger and resentment when we felt that our security or self-esteem was attacked. But a closer look may reveal that we exaggerated the threat. Or we may find that we were depressed because we felt deprived of something we craved. A closer look might suggest that the deprivation was no more serious than not getting ice cream before dinner when we were children. In other words, we wanted something that we couldn't see was not in our best interest. An inventory can help us eliminate some of the anger, resentment, and frustration that we may be harboring. It can help us discover that some of our disappointments and failures may have been caused by our own self-defeating attitudes.

As we do an inventory, we may come across actions we regret, and this may arouse feelings of guilt. Such guilt, which resembles the physical pain we feel when we're injured, can be healthy when it deters us from repeating these acts and leads us to make amends. For those with dual disorders, however, guilty feelings may not always be related to actual misdeeds; rather, such feelings may be a symptom of a coexisting psychiatric illness. Those of us who obsess about guilty feelings with no basis in reality may require special treatment.

While the purpose of an inventory is to enable us to weed out our faulty behaviors, it can also help us discover our character assets. In dual disorders, however, the coexisting illness may render us unable to see our assets; it's only when the proper treatment for the coexisting condition is effective that we are able to do a well-balanced inventory.

How do we put an inventory into action? Just as we would if we were to do a business inventory. We get rid of those products that are unprofitable, and we put the profitable products to the fore. Taking an inventory helps us identify desirable and undesirable behaviors. When we bring them out into the open, we can maximize our desirable traits and try to eliminate the undesirable ones. This brings us to the Fifth Step.

STEP FIVE: *Admitted to God, to ourselves, and to another human being the exact nature of our wrongs.*

Unless we articulate the items on our inventory, the undesirable thoughts and feelings may continue to fester within us and give rise to unhealthy behavior. When we read our inventory to another human being as well as to ourselves and to God, we bring many thoughts and feelings out of hiding and they become more manageable. The person to whom we disclose them must be someone we can trust with our innermost secrets, who can listen to us objectively and be a good listener, and who may help us overcome some of the distorted perspectives we might have about our feelings and actions.

Because a coexisting psychiatric condition may cause anxiety, worry, mood changes, and frustrations whose true nature can be detected only by a trained specialist, we may need help from a competent professional to identify those inventory items based in reality and therefore subject to correction by working the Twelve Steps, and those that are symptoms of the coexisting illness and require treatment.

The coexisting psychiatric illnesses that we've mentioned (e.g., anxiety, panic, depression, or compulsions) are characterized by distressful symptoms but don't constitute a loss of contact with reality. There are, however, psychiatric illnesses, such as psychoses, in which there may be delusional thinking, mania, or hallucinations. Implementing the Twelve Steps must wait until the ability to reason has been restored, lest the delusion or mania distort the concept of powerlessness, a Higher Power, or making an inventory.

Properly working Steps One through Five helps us clarify the various elements of the dual disorder, so that we can make better use of the character-enhancing Steps Six through Twelve. This, together with appropriate treatment, will help us achieve sobriety and emotional well-being.

4

WE AGNOSTICS

Genna L.

FOR MANY of us, Steps Two and Three loom as stumbling blocks. Having acknowledged in Step One our powerlessness in the dual faces of addiction and mental illness, we don't know where to turn to find that power greater than ourselves. Step Two asks that we believe in a Power greater than ourselves; Step Three directs us to turn our will over to God. How can we turn our lives over to God if we firmly don't believe, or even if we are simply uncertain, that God exists?

Yet just as we are not alone in our struggles with a dual disorder, we are not alone in our skepticism or uncertainty concerning the concept of God. Writer Florida Scott-Maxwell describes humanity's ancient search for God:

> In some central part of us mankind must always be trying to understand God. In that poignant core where we call out our questions, and cry for an answer. It is in each of us, even if the question and answer are both despair. We are always talking to God even while we argue him out of existence.*

---

*Florida Scott-Maxwell, *The Measure of My Days* (New York: Penguin Books, 1979), 111.

Those of us with a dual disorder have experienced these moments of despair when we called out to God—unsure if one existed—to be rescued from our illness and addiction, only to be answered with silence, with new days of pain and struggle.

Many of us have indeed argued God out of existence. And why not? Despite our pleas and prayers, the sweeping mood swings or the depression remained, the craving for a drink returned, or the urge to binge became overwhelming again. Over and over again, our mental illness and addiction drew a vicious circle around us, propelling us from one cycle of despair to another.

What was there to believe in? Not only did our personal lives make us doubt that God existed, but the problems of the larger world around us—poverty, homelessness, violence—seemed to reinforce our doubt. The God that may have been presented to us in the religions of our childhood seemed distant and punitive. Traditional organized religion didn't offer the answers to the questions that we asked, on either a personal or a philosophical level. With no response to our needs, no answers to our questions, and no tangible, quantifiable proof that God existed, there was nothing in which we could find faith.

Now, as nonbelievers or skeptics, we are asked to make what initially seems to be an impossible leap of faith: to believe in the possibility that a Higher Power will restore us. Fortunately for us, this leap is not as large or as dangerous as it may initially seem. Since the Twelve Step program was introduced, hundreds of self-described atheists and agnostics have successfully made this leap and begun the spiritual journey of recovery.

The Twelve Step program doesn't ask that we will ourselves into believing something we don't. If you look carefully at Step Three, you'll see that all this program requires is that we turn our wills and lives over to a Higher Power, as we understand that Higher Power. Here is your bridge for that leap of faith. Your Higher Power doesn't have to be God as defined by traditional religion, your friends or family, or even fellow Twelve Step followers. It is up to you to conceptualize and define a Higher Power for yourself.

In order to fully understand and embrace this concept, stop worrying about the existence of God for a minute and just look at the words *Higher Power*. Try to imagine a power or force that is stronger than your individual will. Start with something simple and clear. What about the forces of nature, such as the speeding winds of tornadoes, fierce movement of earthquakes, or rapid sear of a forest fire? Whatever brute strength we possess as individuals cannot compare to the strengths of these natural forces. Earthquakes, tornadoes, hurricanes—these are events we can't control. Instead, we respond to their occurrence. We react by seeking shelter or moving to safety, but we are powerless to stop the force that frightens us.

Similarly, remember the times we promised ourselves (and perhaps friends, family members, physicians, or therapists) with complete conviction that we would take the prescribed medication or would never drink alcohol again? Remember the ironclad determination that we would not let ourselves slide into depression, that we would simply will ourselves into normal, active lifestyles? We have all assured ourselves at one time or another that recovery was a matter of willpower, that if only we could try hard enough, individual strength and determination would conquer our problems.

That resolve shakes and crumbles in the chaos of a manic episode or the desperation of depression. In an instant or after long hours of fighting, we reach for the drink, the food, the drug. It is not that our wills are weak or our resolve artificial. Instead, we are simply powerless over our dual disorder. All of the individual determination in the world will not ward off depression, stop a manic episode, or say no to cocaine. As we do with the tornado or earthquake, we respond to a force we cannot control. The tornado sends us running to basements instead of climbing into our cars to drive to work as we had planned. The single shot of bourbon becomes a whole bottle, the drinking slides us back into depression—the ordinary tasks and pleasures of our lives disappear as our actions once again become governed by our dual disorder.

Acknowledging that powers greater than ourselves exist is an essential movement away from the power of the dual disorder that overwhelms us (the power we've tried to fight and to deny, to no avail) toward the Higher Power that will carry each of us through recovery. This acknowledgment itself requires no faith or belief, simply reason. Is it actually reasonable to believe that any one person is the most powerful force that exists? That no force, power, or knowledge greater than the single human mind exists? From Carl Jung to Albert Einstein, the greatest minds of this century have acknowledged the limitations of the individual mind and speculated about the shape or form that a higher intelligence might take.

Defining the particular Higher Power that will carry each of us through our recoveries is a highly personal and individual right and responsibility. Many agnostics and atheists beginning a Twelve Step program have no desire to discover "God" in the traditional sense. Many people consider their therapists, support groups, or supportive communities their Higher Powers.

Amy, who was bulimic and had bipolar disorder with severe manic and depressive episodes, described the discovery of her Higher Power in these terms:

> I didn't believe in God, or the energy of the Universe, or any of the terms people in my OA group used. But I did believe in logic and education. One day when I was particularly depressed, feeling unable to go on at all, my therapist told me that I didn't need to "muster" up energy or motivation that I couldn't. She said that she could do the work for me for a while, give me the things I needed to continue when I didn't have the power to get them for myself.
>
> It was an incredible relief to give myself over to her expertise and training. She knew how much Librium I needed; she had years of experience working out meal plans that bulimics used successfully. My dual disorder was beyond my ability to understand and manage, but it was not beyond hers.

At this point, Amy let her therapist take over. She accepted the help offered her, the years of training and experience of a professional. This is especially important for people with dual disorders. The interaction of mental illness and addiction can be complicated and volatile. Our therapists and physicians often have powers we do not—the power to prescribe appropriate medication, to unwind and interpret chaotic emotions behind addictive behavior. As people with dual disorders, we can be blinded and bound by their force; professionals who exist outside of the storms of our lives can see clearly when we cannot and can guide us.

The strength we don't have as individuals can also be found in support groups. Many people define their Higher Power as the caring force of community. Jean C. writes about finding her Higher Power in her AA group when she couldn't believe in God.

> This counselor told me to get the attributes of my Higher Power from the group: "The group is going to be your God for a while." So I started watching. What did the group give me besides acceptance? They gave me sharing and caring—I could go on and on about what that group gave me. So today I have a Higher Power that has no eyes, no arms, no face, just a universal power that is filled with love that has mercy on us all. . . . Taking my idea of a Higher Power from the group itself was marvelous. Now my Higher Power has monumental attributes and grows every year.*

Jean found love, support, and something stronger than herself in the people around her. Whereas silence ultimately weakens us and isolation stokes the fire of our dual disorder, opening our lives to people who share the same problems will open each of us to an abundance of love and energy impossible to imagine or describe. People united in a common goal of recovery create powerful communities.

It is important that those of us with dual disorders utilize all available resources for support. Our needs are complex, because we are not dealing with mental illness or addiction alone but with the complicated consequences of the interaction between these two. Sometimes we will need more than one support group in order to create a community that can be called a Higher Power. Our Higher Powers can be personal, combined communities of support groups, therapist, friends, and perhaps family.

---

*Rachel V., ed., *A Woman Like You: Life Stories of Women Recovering from Alcoholism and Addiction* (San Francisco: Harper & Row, 1985), 188.

Atheists and agnostics also find their Higher Powers in things or in ideas. One man decided that a smooth green stone would be his Higher Power. He always carried the stone, and whenever he looked at it, he saw the pain, struggle, and eventual hope that it symbolized for him. During difficult moments, he held tightly to that stone, allowing himself to be carried away by the dream for a better life he saw in its flat green shine.

Higher Powers are as diverse, creative, and unique as the people who define and believe in them. Some people find power in the beauty and force of nature, in putting themselves in perspective as one integral part of our living, breathing planet. Others visualize the God of traditional religion as the infinity of the universe; some of our Higher Powers exist as the tangible energy that guides the world; some see God in a form they're familiar with, such as female, black, Asian, and so on. One woman studied Eastern and Western religions until she had enough information to visualize a power she trusted.

How we define our Higher Power is in our control; our dual disorder is not. Isn't it time, as Larry Eisenberg says in *Night Light: A Book of Nighttime Meditations,* to "resign as general manager of the universe?"* Understand that recovery requires a Power greater than any individual will. Giving our wills and lives to a Higher Power is essential to working the Twelve Step program, essential to recovery.

The Twelve Step program describes turning our lives over to a Higher Power as embarking upon a spiritual journey. Many of us originally cringed at the word spiritual because it reminded us of the traditional religious definitions we'd

---

*Amy E. Dean, *Night Light: A Book of Nighttime Meditations* (Center City, Minn.: Hazelden Educational Materials, 1986).

rejected. However, we are now redefining this awakening to fit our personal definitions of a Higher Power.

The *American Heritage Dictionary* defines *spirit* as "the vital principle or animating force . . . within living beings." This spirit resides in each of us. The spiritual journey we begin by acknowledging a Higher Power is not a journey of sudden conversion or instant religious insight. Instead, recovery itself is the journey. Our spiritual journeys can be the process of unleashing the vitality of life that lies within each of us. This vitality is simply the richness of an authentic and honest existence—an existence directed by our Higher Powers.

The Twelve Step program offers us hope by providing a path out of the chaos of lives ruled by dual disorders. All we need to do is redefine the power that guides our lives. Instead of being overwhelmed by the power of our dual disorders, we are each invited to find a different Higher Power that will guide us through recovery. Our individual Higher Powers can lead each of us as we discover and unleash our individual spirits, our healthy selves.

5

RECOVERY AND RELAPSE

Kate S.

CHAPTER 5 OF THE Big Book of Alcoholics Anonymous, "How It Works," talks about people "who are constitutionally incapable of being honest with themselves. There are such unfortunates. They are not at fault; they seem to have been born that way."* I disagree with these statements. Even the craziest people have periods of lucidity in which they can be honest with themselves, recognize their addictions, work the Twelve Steps, and try for recovery.

To recover, however, a person with a dual diagnosis of alcohol or other drug addiction and mental illness needs a strong support structure. This means not only AA (or another Twelve Step group) but very likely a mental health support group that addresses the disorder from which the person is suffering, such as a manic-depressive group, Overeaters Anonymous, or Emotions Anonymous. For me it meant joining an obsessive-compulsive self-help group. What the obsessive-compulsive group did for me that AA could not was to give me an extended family that understood my limitations, frustrations, and victories in my particular mental illness. I needed most to feel that I was not

---
*Alcoholics Anonymous, 58.

alone, and going to a weekly group helped me realize this.

There are many people with a mental illness. Some of them also suffer from an addiction. I fought for years to prove that I was *not* an alcoholic, only a depressed and suicidal victim of traumatic abuse. Perhaps you've felt this way also. It was only when I reached the absolute bottom of suffering with my drinking that I realized my problem had to be twofold: I was mentally ill *and* I was an alcoholic, and the two were not independent of one another.

I have discovered many things about my dual disorder over the last eight years and one of them is this: I am powerless to control either my mental illness or my alcoholism. One affects the other just as surely as the sun will rise tomorrow. I find that when I am in the midst of a psychotic episode—hallucinating and feeling anxious—I will entertain such strange thoughts as *If I have a drink now, all will be well*, which, of course, is not true. If I drink when I am psychotic, I am doubly likely to think of a way to end my life; if I am *not* going through a psychotic episode and I drink, the alcohol almost always triggers one.

The two disorders are interdependent, and that is why it is a must to find more than an AA group for support. It might be easy to say to AA people that we are some of those unfortunates who cannot get sober, but pulling the wool over the eyes of fellow sufferers (those who are dually diagnosed) is just about impossible.

A therapist is another source of support for people with an addiction and an emotional or psychiatric illness. Whether that person is a psychotherapist, psychiatrist, or psychologist doesn't matter. Whatever works is good. I happen to rely on all three, and over the years I have discovered that just having someone in my corner is a great help in overcoming the problems of mental illness. A therapist can keep me aware of reality, can believe in me when I can't believe in myself, and can either prescribe needed medication or find someone who can. Just knowing they are there and can talk me through a bad time is worth daring to trust someone.

For those of us fortunate enough to have families who understand our illnesses and can offer constructive support, home is also a good place to go when things get overwhelming. A family can be a strong backbone when a bout of mental illness renders us defenseless and inclined to drink or use drugs to feel better. Family members know us well, and they can draw from experience the words we need to hear in order to rally and make it through the bad times.

Friends can do the same work, and for people like me who can't depend on family, friends are the next best thing to a therapist. Many times, when I've been burning my arms with cigarettes, I've called a dear friend in the middle of the night, afraid to go to sleep because I thought I was going to die—and she was always there for me. She may have been a little upset at the lateness of the hour, but she was glad that I trusted her enough to turn to her for help.

And yet, sometimes everything may still seem to fail—AA, mental illness groups, therapists, family, and friends. Things can be going along swimmingly when—Pow!—something seemingly out of the blue strikes, and we are vulnerable to using again.

For example, I recently woke up one morning believing that my medications were depressing me and that alcohol would cheer me up. I thought I could buck all the rules and be happy as a creative drunkard. I heard messages coming through my radio, telling me that I should follow in the footsteps of Hemingway: I could drink and write and probably avoid the crack-up in the end. How wrong I was.

That day I actually drank one can of beer. Immediately following, I saw lights coming through the window aimed at my head. I figured God or something was trying to reach me, so I lay down on the couch and waited. All that happened was that I fell asleep. Nothing more came of the beer except a slight headache when I awoke. I was lucky that time.

The point is this: I was depressed at the time, feeling so bad I really wanted to die, and I thought the alcohol would make me feel good. What it really did was trigger a bout of mania, which ended in more depression. So you see, alcohol and mental illness can affect each other seriously, and the up-and-down roller-coaster ride I go on is a great deal less than fun. The only way to be sure that I am dealing strictly with my mental illness is to stay away from drugs or alcohol. If nothing else, matters don't get so complicated.

Relapse to addiction for the person with a dual disorder can also be caused by problems with medication. I remember that when the doctors were trying to get my medications right, I often turned to alcohol to counteract their side effects. I thought that by using alcohol, I was nullifying the effects of the drugs. What I was really doing was playing a dangerous game of Russian roulette. I should have kept the doctors informed of my state of mind and taken some time off work while the chemicals in my body adjusted themselves.

Now that I am regulated but still have bouts of psychosis, I need constant reminding that I have medications that will help me cope with the upset caused by mental illness. I no longer feel about my medications as I once did—that they are mind-altering and dangerous—but accept that I need to take them in order to be well and to have enough presence of mind to stay away from the drug of my choice.

Another big factor in preventing relapse—one that I forget nearly every other day—is to eat right and get some exercise. Just sitting around the house, hanging on to my state of mind or letting my thoughts whirl, is good for neither my body nor my mind. The prognosis is poor for someone who sits in one place all day, eating or smoking or sleeping. All that sitting is bound to end up in listlessness, and too much time to think or too much extra energy can easily result in a using binge. It's better to get up, stretch, take a walk, or do something that taxes me a little bit. Sedentary and sober don't go together, but exercise and recovery do.

Other things I look at if I find myself close to or in a relapse are my moods. Am I angry? Resentful? Self-pitying? Unable to accept my condition? As addicts we tend to run away from feelings. Before we stopped using, we ran to intoxicating chemicals for help. Now, without them, we're alone with our feelings, and they aren't always pleasant ones. But that doesn't mean they're bad. For every emotion there is a reason, and we would be wise to look into it. Recently I became angry because I have so many psychotic episodes every month. I figured that I dipped low about four times a month. This seemed unfair to me, and immediately I thought of drinking. Thank goodness I didn't. That's one thing about feelings: If you drink to cover them up, they act like bubbles in a water cooler. They always come to the surface.

Another thing I have learned to do is find someone I really trust, and when I get sick I tell that person how I feel and what I want to do, and then I promise not to do anything that is bad for me. Once I wanted to drive my car into the garage, sit there with a bottle of alcohol, and drink until the carbon monoxide got to me. What I did instead was call my best friend, and then my therapist, and tell them what my plans were. Each made me promise to do no such thing, so instead I spent the day reading and listening to music. Just calling someone made me feel as though I had some control over my actions. If I could call someone, then I could avoid attempting suicide. It all made sense. I just had to listen.

Keeping a journal has also been helpful over the years. I found out early that if I wrote down what I was feeling at a given time and then kept writing, I could find my way out of the abyss I was in, just as I did in talking to someone on the phone. (But sometimes keeping a journal worked better than the phone because I had brought *myself* out of the slump and could do it again, anytime, if necessary.) It's a good feeling to keep a journal, and it distracts me from bad feelings I may be having. When I look back on stuff I wrote three or four years ago, I'm amazed at how far I've come.

When things are really going bad and it looks as though I may take up drinking again, the final rabbit I pull out of my hat is to organize my life. I don't mean make a five- or ten-year plan. I mean balancing my checkbook, taking out the trash, catching up on correspondence, entertaining myself with a hobby. There is so much to do in life, but when I am psychotic, I have a hard time remembering that. But if I do something like cleaning, I perk up right away. Keeping occupied is like magic—only better—because there is no illusion involved. It's a safety net in my life, and I've depended on it.

So there really are things you can do to avoid a relapse if you are chemically dependent and mentally ill. You don't have to be terribly creative or smart. Have coffee with a friend, put the loose stamps into your stamp collection, take the dog for a walk, or clean out the refrigerator. This sort of thing may sound simple but, believe me, it may be just the thing to save a sufferer's life.

6

ABSTINENCE AND SOBRIETY

Kate S.

As a person with a dual disorder who doesn't drink or take unprescribed drugs, I must believe that the good feelings will last. And not only that they will last, but that I deserve them.

After I sobered up, I had a hard time believing that anyone could feel so happy. I felt so free, so capable of doing whatever I set my mind to. It wasn't just mania talking to me either. I honestly felt good. The longer I stayed away from alcohol, the more I felt my mental illness seemed to improve.

It is no secret among those of us with a dual disorder that we have what I call a "forgettery." We forget the benefits of sobriety: that without drugs or alcohol, our problems are only "troubles"—which we can manage—and that disasters in our lives can usually be avoided. We forget that after the bad times, there will be better times and that even when the bad times hit, they will not be as bad as they were when we were drinking. Perhaps this is a convenience, but I prefer to think that our illnesses cloud our memories. To compensate, I've placed a huge note on my refrigerator that says, This Too Shall Pass. (You might recognize this as an AA slogan.)

I also have a Post-it™ note on my bathroom mirror to remind me that mental illness and chemical dependency are not separate entities and that sobriety begets stability and stability begets sobriety. The note says, "For every action, there is an equal and opposite reaction." (You might recognize this as one of Newton's laws.)

If you have a hard time believing you are worth the good feelings that come to you when you get straight, you are not alone. I, too, used to believe that I was evil or bad and that I deserved nothing less than death from cirrhosis of the liver. Or I thought a bus should run me over. I've used such logic when I've wanted to start drinking again. I'd tell myself, "What the heck, I don't want to live forever and I probably won't anyway. So I might as well drink and enjoy myself." But was I really enjoying myself? Now that I have enjoyed some sobriety and have awakened in the morning feeling like the day ahead held promise, I know that I was only kidding myself. Nothing feels better than to wake up sober and know I have nothing to apologize for.

With the good feelings, or maybe before them, comes the real understanding that we are not alone in the universe. Sometimes a friend calls us just when we most need it. Or the sun pops out when we're feeling down. Or there's a light and cheerful snowfall. Whatever it is, there is always proof around us that we are not alone. I discovered once again that I was not alone on the night after my last drunk: I got down on the floor next to my bed and prayed to my Higher Power to help me want to live. The next morning I got a phone call from my mother: She just wanted to tell me that she loved me. How simple.

But that's just the way our Higher Powers can work. No one can depend on himself or herself to always be there when the hard times hit. Every one of us needs help at some time. Trust that there is a Higher Power that will carry us when we cannot walk.

As for what *your* Higher Power is—that doesn't matter. I used a little marble turtle for five years. My first therapist gave it to me; I kept it on my bureau and touched it or talked to it when I was having rough times. I honestly believe that the turtle contained a Higher Power. I have heard similar stories of people using glasses cases, light bulbs, or figurines, as well as their AA group. Anything that works is fine. Only you can decide what your Higher Power is.

The most important thing I learned a couple of years ago was that my Higher Power is not an enigma. It works through everything around me. If I'm on the street and a woman comes up to me and says, "Isn't it a great day?" I'm quite sure that it's my Higher Power reminding me to enjoy the world I live in. More than a handful of times I've been sitting in a restaurant and the waitress has come up and told me it's good to see me again. This is my Higher Power reminding me that I am not invisible. It's not mysticism or magic; it's just a series of events to remind me that I am not alone. Most of all we need to know we are not alone.

Down the line there will be a spiritual awakening for you. There is no telling what form it will take. It may be sudden or gradual; no one can tell. But I can assure you that once you have a spiritual awakening, you'll be changed, and there will be something about your recovery that attracts other sufferers.

I was waiting at the bus stop one day when this young man approached me and said, "Hi. I'm a schizophrenic." I was floored, but then I sensed he had approached me for a reason. I rode with him on the bus, and it turned out he was not taking his medication. I tried to tell him this was not a good idea. When he departed, he said simply, "Thank you for talking to me." Helping others can be very rewarding.

The only thing I am cautious about is endangering my own sobriety. I draw the line when it seems someone is trying to talk me into drinking. This I cannot do. In these instances, I remember that it is my job to carry the message, not the alcoholic. If someone who is mentally ill wants to talk to me, I will talk. If that person is sober and wants to stay that way, I will do all I can to support him or her. But first of all, I have to take care of myself; AA has taught me that. My mental illness has taught me to honor my limitations. Keeping my life in order is my job; clearing the shards of temptation from my path is up to my Higher Power. I trust. You will, too.

7
TELLING OTHERS

Jody N.

Personal Relationships

PUBLIC KNOWLEDGE of addiction has become widespread, and telling others about our chemical dependency doesn't pose the same problem in recovery as does telling others about our psychiatric disorder and treatment. Should we tell people who are close to us that we have a dual disorder? Should we inform potential employers or the businesses for which we are working that we have been diagnosed with chemical dependency and a psychiatric disorder or have been hospitalized for a psychiatric disorder? For those of us in recovery from addiction and mental illness, the answers we give to these questions can make a crucial difference.

General guidelines may be proposed as to whether we should tell people about our dual disorder and, if so, when to tell them. But these answers depend upon individual circumstances as well. As stated in the next chapter, "The Stigma of Mental Illness," greater stigma is attributed to mental illness than to addiction.

I would now think twice before mentioning to anyone

that I had been diagnosed with a bipolar disorder, except under the most pressing of circumstances. (However, I don't feel as strongly about mentioning that I am a recovering alcoholic if the subject comes up. Most of the people I know are either in Twelve Step groups or know someone in recovery.) With new friends, I'd wait until a substantial trust level had been reached and I felt that they knew me well before I'd tell them about my breakdown and recovery or that I take lithium (the medication prescribed for mania). I've found that once I've been "labeled" by others or once I've "labeled" myself manic-depressive, it becomes difficult to correct perceptions—often misperceptions—of my behavior. I have only opened myself up to discrimination and prejudice.

By now I've gained enough knowledge of myself, and of how my illness can affect my behavior in some situations, that I'm confident I can handle my own life much as I did before I experienced my first manic episode. I don't need to disclose information about my illness to anyone, and I see few benefits in doing so. Family members understand the nature of my dual disorder, and I can rely upon them in emergencies. In addition, my doctor knows my medical history; by and large, he allows me complete independence, but I can always get in touch with him during a crisis.

When I first found out that the numerous difficulties in my life could be traced directly to a combination of alcoholism and mental illness, I was stunned. The chemical dependency didn't throw me off balance but I panicked when I learned I was also manic-depressive. Creative and artistic circles, with which I primarily associate, are less likely than most of society to be judgmental about mental illness, particularly manic-depression. Nevertheless, I couldn't quite accept that I had been labeled "mentally ill."

This attitude, of course, reflected my own fears and ignorance at the time. I had a disease. I was prescribed medication for the disease, and in my case, I immediately responded to the medication. However, for a couple of years, I told just about *everyone* I met about this illness and what it had done to my life. Now I realize that I reacted in shock.

"You won't ever have to tell anyone about it again," my mother said to me one day, midway through the crisis years of my recovery. (I think it took me a full eight years to feel that I had reached the serenity and acceptance of my past that allowed me to live freely, without either one of my diseases controlling my behavior. At this point, I could approach recovery on a more serene level, without interruption from events that evolved from the major breakdown.) My mother was a wise and discreet woman. She meant my illness was not really anyone's business but she was also assuring me that no one could discern that something was wrong or that I had spent years in turmoil. Medically speaking, taking lithium and not drinking had stabilized my emotions. True, it did take years to process what had occurred in the past as a direct result of an undiagnosed dual disorder, but my life was now stable. No one would suspect a thing. Why tell anyone? Why open a can of worms?

When I did tell others, I discovered that most of these people didn't have much interest in the subject and that the great majority didn't have the ability to understand the nature of my illness. There had been little point in self-disclosure. But I didn't get down on myself for having blurted it out so often. Apparently I had needed to let the world know what I was struggling with until I had reached a plateau in recovery.

In a few instances, telling others did make some sense. My behavior, both drunk and manic, had affected other ndividuals. Telling those individuals about the medical diagnosis helped me to make amends to them. By and large, these people were receptive to the information and understanding about my illness.

The founders of Alcoholics Anonymous recommended anonymity for a reason. Part of the reason had to do with the humility we need to recover from chemical dependency, but surely another part of it had to do with self-protection. For those of us who have been diagnosed with a psychiatric disorder, the goal of recovery should come first; if telling others about your illness will keep you from regaining your full potential in relationships and in work, then don't tell them. Restrict your confidences to your doctor and a few family members and friends whom you can trust to have your best interests at heart.

It may take us years of trial and error to discover whom to trust with such intimate knowledge and when. But when we do find out what works best for us, we'll know also that we have regained our self-confidence and can face a fearful and unreceptive world without jeopardizing our recovery.

A Question of Trust

For those of us who have a dual disorder, learning to trust others, as well as learning to trust ourselves again, may not come easily. Our actions have been influenced by things beyond our control, and it may take time for us to learn our own true motives and trust our instincts again. Trust, a cornerstone of relationships, is likely to have been shattered by our actions during illness. We've done things that the people in our lives found upsetting; most of us have not been reliable in our behavior. Rebuilding levels of trust between ourselves and family and friends will take time.

As we begin to recover (this includes not only our intellectual abilities and physical strength but also our emotional stability and spiritual balance), our friendships and family relationships will naturally improve. People who knew us before our problems developed will be pleased to see us return to the responsible adults they once knew. However, we also need to accept that some relationships may have been damaged permanently. Some people who witness the symptoms of posttraumatic stress disorder, mania, depression, or other disorders may not be able to understand that this behavior was caused by treatable diseases. They may blame us for our actions and may not want to consider the nature of our dual disorders.

For example, when I experienced my manic breakdown, which was exacerbated by chronic alcoholism, I acted in such a way that many people in my professional life thought I was crazy. (Other people just thought that this was the way that writers who drank behaved.) Since then, I have explained to key people the underlying causes of that breakdown, but I wouldn't attempt to explain the disease behind the behavior to others whose relationships are not crucial to me.

As I began to recover and return to the type of behavior that characterized my life before the dual disorder, my family, close friends, and professional colleagues who cared about me could see that the wild extremes of behavior I had exhibited were due to something outside of my control. Prior to my drinking years and my first experience with mania, I had been a controlled, responsible person. When I quit drinking and went on medication, this behavior returned. Obviously, my actions at the height of my drinking and manic episodes had been caused by those diseases, and people could perceive this. They forgave me for actions that had affected them negatively.

But the people who were not intimately acquainted with me before the breakdown didn't have a standard of "normal" behavior against which to judge my actions during mania and drunkenness. I'm not happy about the possibility that they may always perceive me as someone who has little control of her life, but there's little I can do about that except to move on. Were I to return to the profession I once had, I might have to prove myself before my colleagues trusted me on a professional level again; but in most instances, it would seem self-defeating to explain to anyone incidental to my own life what happened.

Early in the process of recovery, when we're getting to know someone, we may want to evaluate levels of trust by asking ourselves the following questions: How long have we known the person? How do we know this person—through work or a social activity? In what context do we hope to have this person in our life—as a friend, lover, or work colleague? Why are we thinking about confiding in this person about our illness?

Once we tell people that we have been diagnosed with a psychiatric disorder, we won't be able to take back that information. We probably wouldn't reveal other intimate details of our lives to most people, unless we thoroughly trusted that they wouldn't use the knowledge against us or use it to judge us unfairly. Unfortunately, considering the stigma surrounding mental illnesses, we'll want to evaluate carefully the reasons and possible repercussions of disclosure.

Some Other Considerations

The backgrounds and life experiences of people vary widely. When someone has had years of experience that might include hardship and tragedy, the likelihood is greater that he or she will place my own experience in perspective.

We may find in the course of a new acquaintanceship that mental illness is an issue in others' lives, too. The bond that results in such acquaintanceship may be similar to the bond formed between people who are chemically dependent— it can strengthen recovery.

Deciding Not to Tell Family and Friends About Our Dual Disorder

Most of us would like to think that family members will support us completely in our recovery, but this may not always be true. Our behavior and actions may have triggered resentments that family members cannot, or do not wish to, forgive and forget.

Our own recovery takes first priority in our lives at all times. Some of these family members may accept us again when we behave in sane and responsible ways. The chapter in the Big Book titled "To Wives"* offers sound suggestions to family members in general. These suggestions also apply to the families of those of us who suffer from dual disorders.

We cannot change other people, only ourselves. The best policy remains to stay guarded around people who can hurt us, even when those people were once close to us. If family members or friends harbor resentments toward us, they may keep us from full recovery.

Sometimes family members will hinder our recovery even though they think they are helping us. We have a dual disorder that isn't easy to understand. Caretaking serves a purpose when we're too vulnerable to fend for ourselves, but we do

Alcoholics Anonymous, 104.

hope to achieve independence eventually. Family members are strongly urged to learn about the psychiatric disorder that afflicts a loved one. Telling family members who cannot or will not understand the psychiatric disorder serves little purpose in our recovery.

I haven't faced these problems with my own family, but I sincerely wish that I hadn't told some people who were once close friends of mine about my illness. For reasons of their own, they used this knowledge to put me down and to keep reminding me that something was "wrong." I had no choice but to drop these friends in order to stay on my recovery course. Had I never told them anything but what was obvious (that I was chemically dependent), I wouldn't have had such painful experiences that held back my recovery. Once I was less sensitive myself to what others thought about my dual disorder, I was better able to deal with those who stigmatized me.

Consequences of Telling or Not Telling Family and Friends

Those of us who have been diagnosed with a dual disorder will need help to recover, and we may face crisis situations that are beyond our control. When that occurs, we'll want someone we trust to be there for us. It's obvious that we need to tell at least one person we trust about our psychiatric disorder; this person should also be aware that we are chemically dependent.

Sometimes we'll make mistakes about those to whom we tell this information. Learning from these mistakes will enable us to gain personal insight into the nature of our disorder and its effect on others.

We live in a time when full public knowledge and acceptance of psychiatric disorders is not widespread. Some disorders are more readily accepted than others. Anxiety disorders, for example, receive popular press more often than other mental illnesses and seem less threatening to others. Also, the severity of psychiatric disorders varies widely. A Vietnam veteran may experience posttraumatic stress disorder in a way that frightens other people; he or she may appear violent. Others who experience PTSD may do so in a way that no one around them notices.

What matters is that we know who we are and how our disorder affects our own lives, so that we can function at our fullest level again. Most of us will be fortunate enough to have one or two people we trust, other than our doctor, and that will be enough for us to fully recover.

Telling People in Your Support Group

There are separate Twelve Step support groups for some of the psychiatric disorders. Each of us will have to make our own judgment about whether or not to tell an Alcoholics Anonymous or Narcotics Anonymous group about our dual disorder. The same general rules concerning trust levels apply in this situation.

Along with medical counsel, Twelve Step support groups can aid us in recovery from a psychiatric disorder and chemical dependency. These groups have become more enlightened about members who have dual disorders, but each group of each fellowship is different. We may want to attend separate groups for both our chemical dependency and psychiatric disorder, unless we are fortunate in finding one group where both can be discussed openly.

Professional Relationships

Should we tell our employers about our dual disorder? Not if we can help it.

That's a simplistic answer to a complicated question, obviously. My own experience leads me to believe that, in general, it's in our best interest to keep knowledge of a dual disorder from an employer. Personally, I've had terrible experiences from telling my employer that I've been diagnosed with bipolar disorder. In any case, whether I mentioned that I was bipolar or not, if I had an episode of mania on the job, I was dismissed.

I've also been dismissed for behavior due to depression; on other occasions, depression, which threatens other people far less than mania, did not result in a job loss for me. Other people have not fared so badly in the workplace (mania is probably one of the most disruptive of psychiatric disorders); whether we mention our dual disorder depends on the type of business, the psychiatric disorder in question, and the duration of our employment.

On the other hand, when I interviewed recently at a theater company, I did mention my bipolar disorder. Because of the many well-known people in the theater and film industries who have been open about their bipolar conditions (Patty Duke, Joshua Logan, and Ted Turner, for example), I felt comfortable mentioning this in response to a question about stress. Bipolar disorder is related to stress, and I don't like to cover up the truth if I can help it.

A negative example of telling people about my condition is illustrated by a recent experience I had when I was working with medical doctors. During my employment interview, I blurted out that I was manic-depressive. This admission didn't keep me from getting the job, but when I began having problems at work that weren't actually related to mania, the doctors interpreted my behavior along these lines. Having stigmatized myself, I'd left my behavior open to misinterpretation. I was eventually dismissed.

For many of us who lose our jobs as the result of a psychiatric disorder, the employment issue is likely to become a minefield, similar to the problems that veterans face in readjustment to civilian life. I have never held a grudge against any employer who has let me go for reasons of mania or depression, although I am usually angry until I find my next job. Recovery from a dual disorder takes years in many cases. I didn't feel that I'd reached a plateau of stability until my eighth year of recovery. Even when I wasn't aware of it, I'm sure that anger and shame and all of the other feelings associated with recovery from addiction and mental illness made me a difficult person to work with. I had been displaced from my primary business and was working in businesses about which I cared little.

Further problems in our recovery stem from financial stress and feelings of dislocation. A Vietnam vet with years of difficulty in readjusting to society, a drinking problem, and PTSD would be an example of someone fighting the odds for an interminable time. I'm not sure that the mental health system or the medical profession provides answers to these problems. We would do better to find support and spiritual acceptance in support groups and in the Twelve Steps.

Finally, when we have been employed for a relatively long period of time under mostly stable conditions and we find ourselves experiencing trouble related to our dual disorder, we can apply the same notions of trust levels to our employers as we do to our friends and family. Seek out someone you trust at your company. If you don't have a colleague you trust, you'll find many larger businesses offer employee assistance programs that can refer you to medical assistance and therapists. Most businesses today understand that psychiatric disorders and addiction are considered medical in nature and may grant you leave or disability pay if you need additional time to moderate your behavior.

If your supervisor or manager points out problems on the job, that person shouldn't attribute these problems to a specific illness; more than likely, he or she is not qualified to do so. A supervisor's responsibility is to isolate the behavioral troubles, and our responsibility is to change the behavior. If the behavior is related to a dual disorder, then we are responsible for our sobriety and for attending to our medical needs.

Once we know that we have a dual disorder, it is our responsibility to break through denial if problems surface again and to seek whatever support we need to correct problems on the job. If we do not and are dismissed accordingly, we need to work through resentments along the lines proposed in the Big Book and honestly assess our roles in causing our dismissal. When, on occasion, we are discriminated against because of our illness and we know that we have done all we can to control our behavior, we may want to seek legal help. What matters most, though, is our recovery and the return of our self-esteem in spite of these employment problems.

Peter J. is an example of someone who has learned to overcome his resentments regarding work. Diagnosed with schizoaffective disorder (a thought disorder with symptoms of affective disorder and schizophrenia) and hospitalized, Peter was able to rebound after his first breakdown and joined AA to maintain his sobriety. He was just out of college and found a job as a staff writer for a magazine. Three years later, when his long-term girlfriend broke up with him, Peter again began to have problems. He was fired from his job and hospitalized again.

After leaving the hospital this time around, he did not have an easy time finding work. There was a recession. Peter found himself working as a waiter, delivering newspapers, doing what were essentially student jobs. His anger over his lost career potential harmed him. He sought counseling to deal with this anger and keep his recovery intact. Although he ended up spending nearly three years doing odd jobs, losing some of them, and facing difficult times because of his situation, Peter eventually regained the serenity he needed to keep his dual disorder in remission.

When he reached this plateau in recovery, Peter was finally able to move on in his career, too. With the aid of grants and loans, he went back to school to pursue his interest in higher education and work toward his Ph.D. He now finds that he enjoys teaching and the flexibility it offers more than he did journalism. In a university setting, people understand his illness to a greater degree, and he can better arrange his time if he starts to experience stress on the job. All things considered, Peter's eventual career change—made as a result of his illness—worked out for the better.

I have yet to meet anyone with a dual disorder who has not experienced severe employment problems. For many of us, these problems began the first time we experienced our psychiatric disorder—before we were diagnosed or had admitted our chemical dependency. One day at a time, we can rebuild our lives, accept our losses, and begin to trust others again.

Matters of the Law

When we are in recovery from a dual disorder, we need to know the employer's legal responsibilities to us and our own responsibilities in regard to the workplace. Some states mandate that employees who suffer from chemical dependency must first be offered treatment under the employer's insurance plan if it is known that problems in the job are directly related to chemical dependency. If the employee refuses treatment and signs a form stating this refusal, then the employer's responsibilities have been met.

It's illegal for an employer to discriminate against us on the grounds of mental illness. What the law states and what employers do, however, are two different things. We want to be honest with ourselves: Are we at a stage of recovery where we can handle the position for which we are applying? If the job is offered to us, will stress on the job, or difficulty fitting in, only add to difficulties in recovery? As much as possible, we want to control employment situations and provide a stable base for our spiritual, physical, and mental health to prosper.

If we feel that we have been severely discriminated against, we may want to seek legal counsel. The Americans with Disabilities Act (ADA) protects us as well as others who suffer from disabilities. We also want to consider, however, how much strife would be involved in taking legal action against an employer. Do we really want to dwell on the situation, or do we want to move on? Again, depending on personal background and type of employment, we will want to discuss these questions with close friends and family or our support groups.

The Employer's Role

The employee who has a dual disorder presents special problems for most employers, depending on the stage of recovery the employee has reached and the amount of self-knowledge and care that he or she can apply to the situation. The Big Book deals practically with the employer's dilemma concerning the alcoholic: "A look at the alcoholic in your organization is many times illuminating. Is he not usually brilliant, fast-thinking, imaginative and likeable? When sober, does he not work hard and have a knack of getting things done? If he had these qualities and did not drink would he be worth retaining? Should he have the same consideration as other ailing employees? Is he worth salvaging?"* It's in employers' best interests to offer the same consideration to those of us who suffer from dual disorders.

Unfortunately, the real disruptions in the work world that occur because of many dual disorders (particularly when someone has not yet faced the nature of his or her diseases, or is in the early stages of recovery) may spell disaster for both the employer and employee.

Falling through the cracks in the mental health system appears to be the rule, not the exception, for people who suffer from dual disorders. Naturally, this makes recovery twice as hard for those afflicted. Except for the most enlightened businesses, the combination of addiction and mental illness seems to be more than they can handle; that once was true for chemical dependency, too. Let's hope that employers of the future will have gained enough sophistication to realize how they can best manage their businesses and retain good employees who have psychiatric disorders.

Alcoholics Anonymous, 139-40.

Some medical doctors will work with companies to assist one of their patients in keeping employment. They will advise the employer to provide what the employee needs to get through a bad time and to perform at the best of his or her ability.

Employers lose the potential of thousands of workers every year by their lack of understanding of mental illness. The situation has improved, but there is still a long way to go.

A Final Word

The medical revolution has already occurred in terms of treatment of psychiatric disorders, but the social revolution lags behind. For those of us who have dual disorders, keeping our serenity in spite of the many grave difficulties that we face in coming back from a dual disorder remains the first priority.

8

The Stigma of Mental Illness

Jody N.

WHEN THE FOUNDERS of AA wrote the Big Book, they understood that they were breaking new ground in declaring alcoholism an illness like—but unlike—any other. "An illness of this sort—and we have come to believe it an illness—involves those about us in a way no other human sickness can. If a person has cancer all are sorry for him and no one is angry or hurt. But not so with the alcoholic illness, for with it there goes annihilation of all the things worth while in life,"* the founders wrote in chapter 2, "There Is a Solution." Since that time, many people have come to understand that addiction is a real disease, and they might not attach a stigma to it. Alcoholics Anonymous itself has become widely accepted and respected around the world.

However, this new understanding of addictive behavior does not seem to translate for many people into an understanding of mental illness; a stigma is still attached. The scientific and medical evidence that psychiatric disorders result from both physiological and environmental causes is as persuasive for mental illness as it is for chemical dependency.

*Alcoholics Anonymous, 18.

But the behavior induced by these diseases seems to invoke greater fear than alcoholic or drug-related behavior. This fear may have two sources: (1) There does not appear to the layperson to be a reason for the behavior. The internal workings of the brain remain invisible, whereas anyone can attribute intoxicated actions to the imbibing of alcohol or the taking of drugs. (2) Some behavior caused by psychiatric disorders is simply less familiar to the public at large. Many people, even those who do not suffer from addiction, know what it is to be drunk. Not as many people will experience a panic episode or a manic episode or a posttraumatic episode. When these behaviors are made more severe by intoxication of any kind, the outward displays of distress are even more exaggerated and may appear violent or terrifying beyond either simple drunken or drug-induced behavior or the manifestation of the other disorder by itself.

Being Called "Crazy"

One sure way to stigmatize mental illness is to apply pejorative terms to the behavior or characteristics of it. We all know the terms people use when they mean to put down or stigmatize someone of another race; being called "crazy" is a similar pejorative for people who behave in the bizarre or unusual fashion that characterizes such disorders as mania, panic attacks, or posttraumatic stress.

Sometimes people use the word to mean merely "strange"; people in artistic circles probably don't use "crazy" in a stigmatizing fashion as often as people in society's mainstream do. Many people who remain vulnerable to changes in brain chemistry or who suffer from other disorders will seem crazy to others. Even family and friends might avoid the afflicted person or penalize him or her for the illness, rather than seek help for the victim.

The stigma of mental illness becomes quite clear when placed in the context of the now relatively familiar disease of chemical dependency. One woman recently diagnosed as manic-depressive wondered what to tell her AA group. Certainly, as the Big Book alludes to quite often, drunken behavior can be considered "insane." But her sponsor, also dually diagnosed, warned her that it would be best not to mention it. "They'll think you're crazy," the sponsor said.

The only reasonable interpretation of this statement is that even when people are enlightened about chemical dependency, someone who has a treatable mental illness may frighten them.

The Stigma of Mental Illness

Historically, people have feared and attached a stigma to the mentally ill and their actions. No doubt people have drunk too much and done foolish things for as long as men and women have populated the world. But the stereotype of the drunk, and the way in which societies have handled public intoxication, seem tame compared to the attitude toward mental illness held by most cultures.

Only recently have organic causes been determined to be the source of most mental disorders. In the past, superstition substituted for science to explain the bizarre actions of people suffering from mental illness. Isolating these people removed them from public sight. Sometimes fear of the supernatural propelled this stigmatization; people truly believed in "demons" and "possession." Often the mentally ill would be treated cruelly by others.

Bedlam, the infamous hospital in nineteenth-century London where mentally ill people wasted away in neglect and abuse, is not far behind us. The discovery that medications could control extreme behavior in people who have disorders of the brain is recent, only decades old. Much of our literature and many of the films reflect the past and the inhumane treatment of people who suffered from psychiatric disorders, causing confusion about the cause and treatment of such disorders even among today's public.

Great intellect is not generally required to understand psychiatric disorders. But the causes and treatment of these illnesses are more difficult for the layperson to comprehend than those of most physical illnesses. What we don't understand, we often fear, and it is this fear that produces prejudice, discrimination, and stigma. (Chapter 2 of this book explains more fully the various psychiatric disorders that precede, accompany, or follow chemical dependency.)

Those of us who are afflicted with a dual disorder need to rise above any stigma that may interfere with our recovery. It may feel like swimming against the tide to do so, but giving in to others' stigmatization will hinder our recovery. When our full potential is again reached, we can help educate the ignorant, if we wish, by being open about our illnesses, thus easing the way for others to recover.

Recovery Must Remain the First Priority

It probably seems that coming to terms with your dual disorder and working through the problems that have resulted in your life are more than enough for one person to handle. However, recovery from a dual disorder is doubly complicated by the misperceptions and ignorance based on outdated notions that society—and perhaps even those close to us—still ascribe to mental illness.

The first priority in recovery is to admit that we have a problem, and that by surrendering to a Higher Power, recovery is possible. In the case of a dual disorder, we must seek medical help as well. For many psychiatric disorders, medications can help to restore equilibrium that no longer can be reached naturally. Neurologists know how the brain works in greater detail today than ever before; but beyond this professional help, most likely you'll need to foster the same type of spiritual acceptance and growth necessary to begin your recovery from chemical dependency.

At this point, too, we may want to admit that we don't control other people's opinions of mental illness and their prejudices regarding it. All we can do is work on the changes we are bringing into our lives. Taking prescribed medication and following the Twelve Steps in most cases will result in perceptible changes in behavior.

The same people who once stigmatized or ostracized us will reconsider their opinions when we change our behavior. Some may not change their minds and may continue to put us down, but that isn't *our* problem. We may not be able to completely control some symptoms of psychiatric disorders; the medication that we need may result in visible side effects that can also create a stigma. Nevertheless, our recovery should depend only on our sense of well-being. People who have been physically injured sometimes live with visible handicaps and learn to function at their fullest potential without appearing to be victims or less than complete human beings.

One way to keep self-esteem high in spite of the obvious problems involved in a dual disorder is to think about the blessings we have in our lives. Some of us have been high achievers in various fields, some of us great athletes—all of us can think of some area in which we've demonstrated capability in the past. It's important not to forget what we are still capable of doing. As the AA founders stressed, recovery takes place day to day. We'll have bad days like anyone else, but it's important to congratulate ourselves on the good things we do and remember the blessings in our lives as we work on recovery.

If we read what the AA Big Book has to say about resentment, we'll see how we can forgive those who continue to stigmatize us or behave badly toward us. Where appropriate, it may help to place into perspective how our behavior might have frightened them or made them wary of us. Making amends to people, as the AA philosophy suggests, may also help in some cases. It's not good to put ourselves down because we have been afflicted with a psychiatric disorder, however. Trying to explain to people how we have recognized that we have an illness and that we have taken responsibility to control it will aid our recovery far more.

The personal stories of those afflicted with dual disorders vary widely. Yet individual stories can help us see our own successes and failures. Overcoming stigma proved difficult for Janet, whose story is told here. But she managed to place into perspective the attitudes of others and to move on with her life.

Janet's Story

A brilliant student all her life, Janet attended college during the 1960s at a large university in the Midwest. She drank, but her drinking didn't seem to interfere with her scholastic abilities or her life. In addition to her good grades, Janet also achieved a reputation as a budding playwright.

When Janet graduated from college, she decided that she wanted to pursue her theatrical talents. She married a fellow student, and while he attended graduate school, she worked at a series of jobs and wrote. Being responsible financially for the family wore Janet down after a couple of years. She started to drink heavily, which strained her relationship with her husband. Janet began to experience symptoms of a breakdown. She had trouble eating and sleeping. Her mind felt as if it were taking off on its own at times. Her husband noticed that now and then her sentences would occasionally trail off. Janet began to panic when she found that she couldn't make sense of her writing—her thoughts simply did not connect. She drank more often in an effort to control these symptoms of her mental and emotional distress.

Eventually, Janet's behavior began to appear strange to others. She had always enjoyed the writing groups to which she belonged. But when she began to approach people at odd moments and talk excitedly in what some perceived as a "crazy" manner, many of her friends and acquaintances at these groups pulled away from her.

"This hurt me more than anything," Janet says now. "I wasn't so out of it that I couldn't tell that they were embarrassed by my behavior. But I didn't know how to stop it." She still recalls the time she entered a rest room during a break at one of her writing groups, and the women there stopped talking when she came in. "I knew they were talking about me. It wasn't paranoia," Janet remembers. Humiliated and ashamed, she withdrew from the groups.

What Janet experienced was stigmatization, being cast out for her actions and being labeled "crazy" for behavior that was eventually diagnosed as symptomatic of a treatable psychiatric disorder. But even the knowledge that she gained of her own illness didn't make the pain of those moments disappear for Janet. Overcoming her resentment and anger at the people who had "thrown stones" at her for becoming ill proved almost as difficult for her in recovery as did learning to manage her psychiatric illness and remain sober.

As her behavior has become modified and stable, Janet has learned not to mention her "breakdown" to most people. They have accepted her at face value; and because her current behavior seems normal to them, when she does mention her illness, they accept it as something that happened in the past. She remains afraid of how they will treat her if she experiences another episode. Most of the people with whom she'd previously associated didn't take the time to reconsider their opinion as Janet became well, and she didn't try to force herself back into their circles.

"I think it made me a more compassionate person," says Janet. "I am more conscious now about not judging people on external appearances. I know what it must be like to be a minority, to be fat, to be an outcast in this society. Others' ignorance only reflects their own insecurities, but I wish they knew what pain they caused me when all that was wrong was something that could be treated by medication, hard work, and understanding on their part."

Coming to Terms with Stigma

No one really wants to be different from others. Insecurities cause all of us to seek out others who'll accept us as we are. If, for one reason or another, we find that we're in a group of people who ostracize or stigmatize us for our psychiatric disorder, here are a few approaches to keep recovery ongoing.

Try to understand their point of view. Do they fear the illness because it reminds them of someone they once knew? Remember, it is only recently that research into mental illness has caused great strides in understanding and treatment. A social revolution lags far behind this research.

Are they critical because they need to put down someone who seems vulnerable? We can't change the world, only ourselves. People who stigmatize others are best left alone. We may encounter bullies now and then; it is best to steer clear of them.

Think of taking the same approach advised in the AA Big Book if your behavior during an episode is the reason that someone has made judgments about the illness. Make amends in that case, but only if doing so will not harm you or the other person.

Finally, keep in mind that our own prejudices may cause us to be overly sensitive to remarks by other people. We may be far more conscious of the illness than others actually are, and we may read our own fears into their comments and actions.

Try listing your fears in regard to your mental illness. What are the causes of these fears? What is the truth about the illness that you have learned in your recovery? If you give others a chance, you may find them far more forgiving than you have been of yourself for the unfortunate circumstance of being diagnosed with a dual disorder.

Sometimes our own fears can keep us from treating and preventing outbursts of our illnesses. In some cases, this leads to tragedy. Ginny's story shows how one woman's oversensitivity to what others might think led to a preventable outcome.

Ginny's Story

Ginny's life began falling apart when she was thirty-six. In her early thirties, she had been diagnosed as having an anxiety disorder, characterized by panic episodes with resulting agoraphobia (fear of public places or places from which it seems difficult to escape if needed). These two disorders often go hand in hand; the person who is vulnerable to panic episodes (a feeling of being out of control, marked by difficulty in breathing and a fast-beating heart) often feels ashamed of them.

Although Ginny took her prescribed medication, she drank heavily as well. She drank because she thought it made her feel more relaxed; in fact, drinking only increased her anxiety. Ginny had always made her own way. Maintaining control over her family and home seemed to her the only thing that mattered; what she couldn't admit was that the illusion of control masked the terrifying feelings she had of losing control altogether.

Most of her friends perceived Ginny as a tough and practical businesswoman. Tall and striking, she had experienced two failed marriages. With men, as with her friendships with other women, she masked any vulnerability. Ginny knew she had a problem with her panic episodes and knew that alcohol was beginning to take over her life. She thought that if she talked about her fears and insecurities, however, her friends and family would think she couldn't hold her life together. The truth was that Ginny regarded her problems with more shame and fear than anyone else did.

No one had the nerve to confront Ginny with concerns about her drinking once it became apparent that she was losing control. They knew how much it meant to her to be making it on her own. Until she lost her job at an advertising agency, Ginny lived a lie successfully.

But with the loss of her job and subsequent repossession of her home and car, Ginny began to cave in. The slide downhill was quick. Even when her ex-husband petitioned for and won custody of their son, Ginny could not cry for help. She already felt stigmatized as a divorced mother by society, and her imagination led her to believe that people would think her crazy if she sought the hospitalization she needed.

Soon, all Ginny could feel was humiliation and a sense of powerlessness, but she blamed those feelings on a society that didn't treat women with respect. Two suicide attempts—the signal of a person who is out of control taking control the only way he or she can—and an emergency hospitalization still couldn't persuade Ginny to change.

Finally, Ginny's life did end with an overdose of pills and alcohol. On the night she died, she apparently also experienced a panic episode and ran into the hallway of her apartment building, where she collapsed. She had tried to call for help, but it was too late.

Ginny's fears about stigmatization were not irrational; certainly there are many people who wouldn't have understood the menace of her dual affliction and the struggle to come to terms with her illnesses. They might have blamed her for her failures.

But those who loved Ginny had always seen that behind her tough exterior, there was a scared and vulnerable young woman. They admired Ginny for who she was as a person and would have supported her in recovery, hoping to find once again the loving mother, daughter, and friend they had known.

Conclusion

If we had chronic diabetes and chemical dependency, or if we were chemically dependent and afflicted with chronic heart disease, we would probably not hesitate to get help and follow a prescribed medical plan to maintain our health. Most psychiatric disorders aren't much different from physical illnesses such as diabetes. Accepting that fact ourselves, and helping others close to us accept it, will result in our recovery from a dual disorder if we also follow the Twelve Steps of AA.

People who are threatened by our behavior when we're ill, or who cannot or will not understand, won't really matter to our recovery if we choose not to let them. Ultimately, no one can take away our dignity. As we become honest with ourselves and gain peace of mind—putting our past actions into perspective and learning to differentiate between our dual disorders and our true selves—others will begin to see us in a different light as well.

Being aware of the many people in our society who learn to cope with being stigmatized for things beyond their control may also help us recover our self-esteem. Some other illnesses, such as AIDS, also carry stigmas. Although mental illness afflicts millions of Americans (some estimates state that at any one time, more hospital beds are being used by people who suffer from emotional or mental illnesses than physical), people in the past haven't talked openly about psychiatric disorders. Secrecy and mystery shroud these illnesses the way they once did alcoholism.

Taken literally, *disease* means "without ease." Who can argue that a person whose mental balance has been unhinged and his or her basic character changed is not without ease? Fortunately, we know far more about mental illness now than ever before, and if we attend to our spiritual recovery as well as our physical one, we stand a good chance of regaining an even better life than the one we previously knew.

Vincent Van Gogh suffered from a mental illness, manic-depression. Almost certainly his drinking exacerbated his episodes of mania. Van Gogh himself understood the reality of what it meant to be afflicted with an illness that ended up controlling, and ultimately taking, his life.

He wrote to his brother, Theodore, "If somebody says to you: 'you are ill,' that does not help you much, but if he says, 'do this or that and you will recover,' and his advice is not misguided, that is the thing that will help you."*

For ourselves and those who care about us, what remains important is that we receive help and follow it to the best of our ability—not that we have been, or may again, become ill. Don't give stigma credibility, and it will disappear as we move on with our new lives, stronger for having come to terms with a dual disorder and achieving serenity despite all the obstacles in our path.

---

*Mark Roskill, ed., *The Letters of Vincent Van Gogh* (New York: Atheneum, 1963), 131.

9

TO THE FAMILY

Paula Phillips, M.A., A.T.R.

Questioning Our Fate: A Strength in Adversity

AS FAMILY MEMBERS, we are assailed with two questions when we hear that our loved ones suffer from serious and potentially long-lasting mental health and chemical use problems: *Why?* and *What did we do wrong?* We long for answers to these troubling questions, and we long to understand our contribution to their suffering. This is admirable, a testimony to our care and concern for others. Ideally these questions would guide us to learn new ways to resolve problems and to live our lives. But questioning ourselves about the cause of our loved ones' coexisting mental health and chemical use problems and our role in their evolution is often transformed from a strength into a punishment when it's accompanied by shock, confusion, fear, shame, anger, and grief. These feelings are common to people who are challenged by unexpected and distressing situations. Initially it's a relief to know a name and a diagnosis for the altered mood, thoughts, and behavior of a loved one in the throes of an acute crisis. Yet these words may also confirm a reality we don't want to be true, a reality that sentences our loved ones and ourselves to an uncertain future.

Beyond Shame and Abandonment

Our natural need to be strong, whole, and in charge of the direction of our lives interferes with open acceptance of this uncertain future. Whether we discuss with others or speak quietly to ourselves about what has happened, we feel the stigma, our collective shame of being flawed, weak, and vulnerable. We fear the disapproval and judgment of others. We pull away from our loved ones as if their problems were contagious, and thus we risk abandoning them when they most need our support and affirmation of love.

Maintaining the illusion of normalcy becomes a cruel master and promotes the abandonment of our loved ones on many levels. We may deny the truth of their dual disorders and attribute their behavior to more socially acceptable causes, such as immaturity, stress, low motivation, or hanging around with the "wrong" crowd. We may discourage open discussion by changing the subject when our loved ones describe their problems and experiences with treatment. We refuse involvement in their treatment for fear of how we may be judged. We may cut off contact with them in an attempt to protect ourselves from the impact of their immediate distress and the enduring challenge of learning once again how to live in the face of limitations. And in that abandonment, we lose our loved ones and ourselves. Fortunately that abandonment need not be permanent, especially if we allow ourselves to be gently guided by the questions *Why?* and *What did we do wrong?*

From "Why?" to Understanding and Support

Asking *Why?* directly and openly encourages us to participate in the suffering and recovery of our loved ones. Having the courage to pursue information in the face of our fears and worries will ultimately lead to answers that may comfort us. A wonderful place to start is to ask our loved ones, "Tell us what it's like for you," and to wait to hear their answers. It is so easy to judge, much harder to listen and learn, yet that is what is required of us. In addition, we are challenged to set aside our need to take charge and return life to "normal." We may need to readjust our expectations and hopes for our loved ones and families.

We may also find answers to our questions through reading and other people. Medical, mental health, and chemical health professionals offer individual appointments and informational presentations in many settings. But it's up to us to set aside our feelings of shame, embarrassment, anxiety, and fear, and to ask what we want to know about our loved ones' dual disorders. Professionals are often willing to share what they know and to direct us to other educational opportunities in our communities. But you might not be able to participate in the treatment process. Rules on confidentiality and privacy of treatment often interfere with family involvement in the treatment process. Our loved ones may choose to pursue their treatment independent of our participation. Don't despair. We can still seek answers to the question *Why?* for ourselves. If we communicate our desire to understand and to learn for our own benefit, we open doors to professionals. They may not be free to talk about our loved ones specifically, but they can share current information about dual disorders and provide suggestions to promote greater health for our loved ones and for our families as a whole.

Our loved ones' mental health and chemical health problems can isolate us from our families and communities. But there are support groups to provide us with information and opportunities to learn through a compassionate acceptance and understanding of our suffering. Other people become a balm to our wounds; they can help us see that our preconceptions of mental illness and chemical dependency were based more on our distress than on reality. Our isolation dissolves when we talk about shared experiences and exchange practical suggestions for getting on with the business of living with our suffering loved ones.

These support groups are often sponsored by hospitals, outpatient clinics, advocacy groups, churches, and other community agencies. Some groups focus on educating family members in a structured format about mental illness and chemical dependency; others focus on support, with group facilitators providing information requested by members. Some groups are facilitated by professionals, others by family members. Disappointment may tempt us to give up on our search for answers and support. But we must be patient and willing to try more than one group until we find one that meets our needs. A commitment to regular attendance may multiply the benefits for ourselves and our families.

From Self-Blame to Confidence

Implied in the question *What did I do wrong?* is the personal blame we assume for our loved ones' mental health and chemical health problems. Turning inward we search our memories for times when we may have failed our loved ones. And being human, we discover time and time again our imperfections in past interactions. Convinced that their suffering is our fault, we may punish ourselves by listing all of the "If only I . . ." times, times we wished we had behaved differently. Tempting as it may be to blame ourselves, it's essential that we stop tormenting ourselves. Punishing ourselves with thoughts of our own failure will not change the reality of our loved ones' dual disorders. Self-blame is actually one of the many forms of denial we may experience. If we persist in searching within ourselves and our families for the cause of the dual disorders, we will thwart our efforts to learn what has happened and how to cope with the situation. Effective behavior in the present depends on our grasp of the following fact: *Families are not the cause of mental health and chemical use problems.* The question *What have I done wrong?* is best used to motivate us to learn what to do to influence the course of the dual disorders in the best way possible.

As we move from denial to acceptance, we will be challenged to transform the urge to blame into the excitement of discovering untapped strengths and resources within ourselves and our families. We will ask instead, *What can I do to promote the functioning of my family?* and *Where can I learn the skills that will help me accomplish this goal?* The emotional turmoil will fade as we develop confidence in our newfound skills to solve problems, manage crisis situations, and communicate more effectively. Shame will turn to pride as we develop our ability to shed old habits and learn new behaviors that promote a more stable and joyous family life. Trusting the goodwill of other people, we will turn to professionals and support groups to encourage the development of these attitudes and skills. Relief and comfort will come as our questions are addressed in these open discussions of dual disorders. As we enter into supportive relationships, we will develop greater openness to new ideas, new behavior, and new experiences. The compassion and kindness we free in our hearts may lead us to advocate in our communities for more understanding and humane treatment for individuals suffering from dual disorders and for their families. Mental illness and chemical dependency begin as unwelcome strangers in our homes. Our lives are disrupted and chaotic. We forget how to laugh and recognize the joy in our lives. Painful and ugly emotions direct our decisions and behaviors as the love we have felt for our loved ones is challenged as never before. Like children frightened of the dark, we close our eyes and pull the covers over our heads, hoping against hope that this crisis will go away. Yet morning fails us, we don't get that wish, and things don't magically return to normal. Shame and ignorance push us into greater isolation. It is tempting to close our eyes and sever the bonds of affection to our treasured loved ones. Our learning stops and life goes on, somewhat reduced. But we can choose to open our eyes to the reality of our situations and, in our pain, rediscover our joy and resilience in crisis. Questions that plague us will be answered as we push ourselves beyond denial. We will learn how to take care of ourselves, our loved ones, and our families with skill and warmth. Our eyes will see and our hearts will reach out to welcome those suffering from mental health and chemical use problems back into our families and our communities.

Personal Stories

Our stories disclose in a general way
what we used to be like, what happened,
and what we are like now.
ALCOHOLICS ANONYMOUS

ALAN'S STORY

M Y NAME IS ALAN. I am thirty-two years old, a recovering phobic and alcoholic. I also suffer from anxiety and panic-related disorders.

Looking back at my childhood, which wasn't very happy, I can recall always feeling a little different from other kids. I was always nervous, afraid of elevators, closed-in places, open spaces, and people. I used to hyperventilate a lot. I was often afraid that my bladder would lock up on me and I wouldn't be able to urinate. Sometimes I would let a little urine seep out, just to be sure that my bladder was working. This caused a lot of embarrassment. Then there were times I was very conscious of my heart beating. Sometimes I thought it was beating too slowly and then sometimes it would race out of control or even beat irregularly.

When I was fourteen, all hell broke loose. I experimented with hashish one day, and my brain went into chaos. Things around me no longer seemed real. My body went numb. My mind detached from my body. I fell into a complete state of panic. I didn't know what was happening to me, and I was unprepared. I thought that if this was what it was like to be high, I wanted no part of it. After a couple of hours, reality finally returned, but only by reading and praying could I bring myself out of the panic. Reading and praying would become tools to bring me out of panic stupors in the future.

About a year later, I married a girl I'd gotten pregnant. And then all the feelings I'd experienced a year before in that drug-induced panic returned.

I was at a local shopping center when, out of the blue, it hit me, a full-blown panic attack. I had jelly legs; my heart was racing and pounding; and I was sweating, dizzy, and becoming detached from reality again. *Why is this happening now?* I thought. *I haven't taken any drugs. What is it?* My thoughts were like the winds of a hurricane. All I could focus on was that I had to get home. I left my groceries in the checkout line and ran out the door. At home I finally started to calm down and reality began to return. *My God, what is happening to me?* I screamed. I remember telling myself not to tell anyone about this; they would think I was crazy and lock me up in some mental institution.

The next day in school, I thought about what had happened the night before. The more I thought about it, the more I could feel my heart start to gallop. I imagined it galloping right up from my throat and out my mouth. I wanted to get up and tell the teacher, but my legs wouldn't move. The harder I tried, the weaker they got. It felt like I was having a heart attack and was paralyzed. But I managed to get up, stumbled to the teacher, and collapsed into her arms. I finally managed to say, "I think I'm having a heart attack." I was rushed to the emergency room and diagnosed as having a "nervous disposition" with "light anxiety." Cause: unknown.

Thus started a series of panic attacks, anxiety attacks, suicidal tendencies, and a drinking and drugging lifestyle that would last for seventeen hellish, torturous, terrifying years.

At sixteen and seventeen, I couldn't leave my house; I was too afraid to go out. I was newly married, with a child, and I couldn't even work. I was always fearful that the "big one" would hit. The house was my safety zone, but I was a prisoner of my own mind. It was at that time that I first thought of suicide; I thought I could escape the inescapable. I sat with a loaded shotgun at my head, ready to pull the trigger, while praying to God for relief. I was prepared to hear the tip of the hammer on the firing pin, but I only heard the tapping at the door. It was a friend of mine coming to talk about some anxiety that he had been experiencing recently. Coincidence or what? I don't know, but this was the first of many reprieves that were to interfere with my obsessive suicidal thoughts. Suicide, it seemed, was the only control I had over my life, the only way out of my prison of mental torture. I now know that God had been intervening.

Over the next year, I pulled myself out of my depression somehow, just enough to start a new job at a factory making tires. I thought I had finally gotten hold of my life and that things would be okay from then on.

About twelve months into the job, the disease hit again. I felt crazy. I was missing too much work because of anxiety and panic attacks, and the company was threatening to fire me. Thinking my heart was causing all of my panic attacks, I went to a heart specialist. I underwent many tests. I couldn't finish the treadmill stress test; I thought I would surely have a heart attack and die if I did, because my heart was already racing a hundred miles an hour. I told the doctors that my legs wouldn't hold up and I had to quit. (This was one of the many lies I would tell just to survive, because no one understood this freaky disease.) The tests indicated that my heart was as healthy and strong as an ox, that the irregular and racing heartbeat was the result of stress. (*Shit, I thought, the crazy heartbeats are due to some unknown disease and I'm dying.*) Referred to a psychiatrist, I got counseling, prescriptions for minor tranquilizers, and reassurance that my problem was common and would go away. I was told that beta blockers and tranquilizers should do the trick. But none of this explained my feelings of total panic, detachment, and unreality.

Well, the panic went away, only to come back a few days later with unmerciful vengeance. Soon I realized I couldn't handle the attacks anymore. I lost my job. *What did I ever do to deserve this form of torture?* I cried. *Is God punishing me for something I did in the past?*

I went from doctor to doctor, psychologist to psychiatrist, looking for a cure. But there was none.

A couple of years earlier, I had experimented with alcohol, and I recalled that it had brought temporary relief. Now I thought, *What if I drink constantly? Won't that ease the anxiety?* I rationalized that this had to be true, and alcohol became the escape mode that I prescribed for myself over the next fourteen years. The more anxiety I experienced, the more I slipped into the grasp of alcohol. I didn't realize it at the time, but alcohol was the cause of the increase in anxiety and panic attacks.

These years brought drunkenness, more suicide attempts (six to be exact, some nearly fatal), accidents due to alcohol, my abuse of my family, and, finally, divorce from my wife. I lost countless jobs because of the panic attacks. I couldn't function any longer. I was labeled as "just a lazy excuse for a human being" who didn't want to work and who used anxiety as an excuse for not working. (I think panic disorders are harder on men in this respect, because society looks on men as people who should never cry or have mental problems and who should always hold a job, no matter what.)

Finally it became impossible to hold any job for long because of the panic attacks. So I signed up for disability and got it. (I had lost so many jobs that it was obvious I really did have a problem.) But I soon realized that not working wasn't the answer either—inactivity just brought on more depression. So I figured I would just lie back and wait; I'd just drink myself to death. But it didn't work that way. I was slowly losing my sanity by drinking and using drugs.

Then I made another suicide attempt, earning another trip to the psychiatric ward. There I finally found a name for my problem when the psychiatrist handed me a book on anxiety disease. I was ecstatic and relieved. I finally knew what I was suffering from.

The book explained that I had a real disease, a disease that was coming from within, not just everyday anxiety. With this information in hand, I could hold my head high and claim that I wasn't just a lazy, rotten human being, but that I had a real disease. I wondered how I was going to bring it under control, although, in a way, I didn't care, for I was being held prisoner by alcohol and tranquilizers.

It all came to a head the year I turned thirty-one. First I got a DUI in January, and I made my sixth suicide attempt in June. The seventeen years of torment, panic, and alcohol abuse had taken their toll. My health was failing. My sanity was all but gone. The doctors were talking about having me committed. I was driving my family further apart from me. My depression had fallen to a new low. Life wasn't worth living. The demons in my mind were having their way.

I don't know exactly why, but I started to feel spiritual at this time. Perhaps I had hit bottom. Perhaps God had seen that I had finally had enough. I came to believe that there had to be be a way out, a *positive* way out. I wondered what my purpose in life had been and what it would be. I sensed God's presence around me. I felt a fire in my heart—not panic this time, but a glow of desire, because I truly did have a purpose. I felt that my suffering had not been in vain but that I had experienced it for a reason.

I checked myself into a substance-abuse treatment center to embark on a new journey, a new plan from God for my life. While there, I was introduced to Phobics Anonymous (PA). I decided to put my effort into this program as I'd never put effort into anything before; I'd finally found my purpose in life. I met others in PA who were suffering as much as I was. God brought us together to help each other with one common problem: the debilitating effects of panic disorders.

My life has improved miraculously since coming into PA six months ago. These have been the most serene and the happiest months of my life. My depression is lifting. My zest for life is returning. My sanity is back. My self-esteem and confidence are high. I'm going back to college. I'm going back to work. I'm off all tranquilizers but one, which I take only as needed. I'm going places I couldn't go before. I'm no longer afraid of people, places, and things.

By working the Twelve Steps of PA, I've gotten rid of my old negative ideas and catastrophic ways of thinking. I've gained a feeling of control over my life, not fear. Before Phobics Anonymous, I would gather evidence for why I should die; I now gather evidence for why I should live. I'm learning how to pray and meditate; I'm changing my diet;

and I'm regularly saying positive affirmations, visualizing change, going to counseling, and improving my relationships. I recognize that many of my anxieties stem from resentments, so I am learning to forgive those people I resent.

Through PA, I'm also developing the courage to make changes and the honesty to share my secrets and problems with others. I realize it's an ongoing process, learning who I am; developing goals; and learning to love myself and to let go of my addictions, obsessions, faulty coping techniques, negative behavior, and self-defeating attitudes.

I know that I will experience some anxiety, but it's okay. Accepting myself, thinking positively, keeping good company, practicing love, and expecting miracles are now part of my life.

To paraphrase something I read somewhere: "I feel that providence, nature, God, or the power of creation seems to favor human beings who accept and love life unconditionally."

The universe supports me, and I am worthy of that support. All I can say now is "Free at last, free at last, free at last." Thank God and PA, I am free at last.

Daile's Story

"Hi, I'm Daile, and I'm a survivor." That's how I identify myself at meetings. I am recovering from multiple personality disorder (MPD) and alcoholism. My therapist and I believe that I have been "multiple" since toddlerhood, and I believe I've been alcoholic since I was very young. I've come to accept that I have an addictive personality: If "it" changes how I feel, I will use it and abuse it—whether it's alcohol, medication, food, or activities. My recovery has been a long, continuing process that has relied on the Twelve Steps to begin healing the effects of my abusive (incestuous) childhood.

I began drinking when I was still struggling to accept my diagnosis of multiple personality disorder. I was trying to stifle the pain of the returning memories of my violent childhood. Within three months, alcoholism had me at a bottom—driving drunk, lying to friends and family, stealing money for alcohol, passed out in my own vomit, drinking large amounts of booze while on psychiatric medications.

At twenty-eight, a mother of three, I was about to lose it all. My husband was threatening divorce, and I was contemplating suicide. My system of personalities was in turmoil.

The body was out of control. Alcoholics Anonymous felt like my last hope of gaining any control over my need to drink. I had no expectations of learning a new way to live through the program—I simply wanted to stop drinking.

The first thing I did in those early AA meetings was to "yeah, but . . ." everything I heard. I knew that no one there could understand my pain, my struggle to heal from my abusive past, my many personalities. I was different.

Then I met Al. Al was a fixture at area meetings. He had seventeen years of sobriety and a gentle way of seeing the winner in everyone. He encouraged me to talk about whatever it was that continually compelled me to dive headfirst into an alcoholic haze. Al always spoke of the Twelve Steps not as simply a way of not drinking, but as a way of living. It was from Al that I first felt complete acceptance. It was the first step toward the personalities accepting each other.

Al was the first AA member that I ever told about the multiplicity. He didn't bat an eye, saying, "Just teach the Steps, the program, to *all* of you." He made it sound so easy, so acceptable. That's what I did: All of the personalities learned to live the Twelve Step way of life to the best of their abilities—even the children.

Al taught me the simple things: how to use the Serenity Prayer to regain my focus and curb anxiety attacks. How to cope as sometimes the only woman in a room of two dozen men. He urged me to break One Day at a Time into One Minute at a Time, if that was what I had to do to avoid drinking. When I nearly stopped attending meetings because of my reaction to touch, Al supported my decision to wear a name tag that read, "I am an abuse survivor—please don't touch me." All the handshaking and hugging triggered memories of physical and sexual abuse. As I felt safer in the fellowship of my home group, he encouraged me to grow past the name tag and to risk giving and accepting touch.

In the early days of my sobriety, I thought that I'd never manage even a week of sobriety. One of the personalities would always blow it, and there we'd be, starting over. And how could I explain it to anyone? It sounded like an excuse: "Well, I 'woke up' and I'd been drinking—but it wasn't me." Convenient, right? It felt like I was living one lie after another. After all, I wasn't sure that *I* believed I was multiple—how could I expect anyone else to understand?

But one personality, Berta, consistently attended the meetings and really began the process of learning the Steps and teaching them to the rest of us. Al encouraged Berta to have her own sobriety date, so we observed two dates—one for Berta and one for the physical body.

The physical-body sobriety date was important for medical reasons. My family doctor, who followed the progress we made toward sobriety, was always concerned about the effects of the alcohol and the medication prescribed by the psychiatrists. I was on a merry-go-round of antidepressants, antipsychotics, and major and minor tranquilizers. Nothing worked for very long—which is common for multiple personalities. And it was difficult to be certain that the medication was taken properly. At one time, several personalities all thought it was their responsibility to take the medicine—so they would each take a dose. Eventually, the body would react to the unintentional overdosage. Sobriety was not maintained.

Once I arrived very drunk for an appointment with the psychiatrist who prescribed medications for me. He asked me if I had been drinking. I said yes. Nevertheless, I walked out with prescriptions for a month's worth of antidepressants and a tranquilizer. This doctor didn't accept my therapist's diagnosis of MPD, and he knew that I was alcoholic and addictive.

It was the fourth and final psychiatrist who validated my therapist's diagnosis of MPD and prescribed medication that took into account that I was alcoholic and addictive.

Up to this point, I hadn't done much work on my relationship with my Higher Power. Oh, I was doing the standard AA routine of starting and ending the day in prayer. But in the face of the returning memories, it was difficult to believe that my HP cared about me. And it was about to get worse.

First, my husband's job situation forced a 160-mile move away from his family (our major support network), my AA and ACA (Adult Children of Alcoholics) recovery families, and my therapist. Second, word came that I had been denied medical insurance. I tried to stay grateful, as the program taught, but it was difficult—no, it was impossible.

The months of re-establishing my family and adjusting to a new job, a new home, and the kids' new schools left little time for my recovery. I had to find a new therapist (I'd had enough of psychiatrists) who would see me with no insurance at a reduced fee. I had to learn to manage my life without medications. I had to build a totally new support network. I cursed my Higher Power on a daily basis while attending meetings and wearing a "working the program" mask.

But I did find a therapist. And I did continue to attend meetings, although by this time, I had switched from AA meetings to ISA (Incest Survivors Anonymous). By now I had discovered feelings, and I felt unaccepted and judged by the conservative AA belief that my anger and pain indicated I was a "dry drunk." Some of the AA doctrine taught in my new AA meetings was in conflict with my therapy—yet I wanted and needed the Twelve Step program in my life. For me, ISA was the answer.

Throughout this process, I recognized that I didn't simply need to not drink, I needed to heal the pain that I was attempting to medicate with alcohol, food, and so on. My tools for healing became the Twelve Steps, the slogans, the Serenity Prayer, the belief in a Higher Power (even while cursing him), the support of the fellowship, and work with an excellent therapist.

On my one-year anniversary, Al died of brain cancer. I drove three hours to his funeral, wishing I could go with him. There is no doubt in my mind that the caring of this one man laid the foundation for my recovery. He believed in my ability to heal. He accepted me—all of me. He patiently taught me the Twelve Step program, as he understood it. He encouraged me to seek a relationship with my Higher Power—even if it was still one of anger and questioning. He never judged me or my program.

I am now in the process of final integration of all of my personalities and fragments. I am by no means finished—there is no graduation to health. I will always struggle to avoid dissociating when I am stressed. I will always have an addictive personality. But the Twelve Steps have indeed become a way of life for me: When I suffered from stress-induced amnesia during the therapy session that led to final integration of my multiple personalities, I remembered the slogans and promises first—before the names of my husband and children.

Today I am Daile, a recovering alcoholic with quality sobriety time and an integrated multiple personality. I like to believe that somewhere Al is smiling and saying, "I knew you could do it—I said you were a winner all along."

DONNA'S STORY

HERE'S MY CURRENT situation: I've been married for almost twenty-three years and have three sons. My husband is a recovering alcoholic; he went through treatment but did not go to AA or therapy. I just turned forty. I've been sober now for thirteen years, smoke-free for nine years, free of bulimia for eight years. Last but not least, I am managing a mental illness called *cyclothymia* (mood swings).

My family background goes like this: My mother is a chronic paranoid schizophrenic. I am the second oldest among three brothers. From age four on, I lived with one set of grandparents or the other. Social workers would visit from time to time. My mom was in and out of hospitals. I was afraid of her frequent personality switches. I didn't learn how to cook, clean house, or even babysit. I was afraid most of the time and never talked about it.

When I was fourteen, I took my first drink. I didn't like the taste of alcohol and had a hard time keeping it down, so I tried it only a couple of times. In those days, I was always on a diet, although when I look back, I really wasn't overweight (but flat stomachs and Twiggy were in style). Just before I turned fifteen, I gave up my virginity to my eighteen-year-old boyfriend. It was painful, both physically and emotionally. I felt guilty. I knew I was too young, but I told myself I was in love.

Then I began to drink again and found the escape I needed. If I didn't drink on the weekend, I felt the whole week was a loss.

I learned a couple of things early on in my drinking. I learned that if I wasn't with my boyfriend, I would flirt and do things I would later regret. Then, and throughout my drinking career, I always got sick and vomited; sometimes I would put a finger down my throat to help. I also did this when I was nauseated (which was often). I realized that there was a payoff to these episodes—I felt thin—so it was worth it!

Eventually I broke up with my boyfriend to go out with Bill. By the end of my senior year of high school, at age seventeen and a half, I was three months pregnant. So Bill and I got married that June and lived with my in-laws for thirteen months. He worked five to seven days a week, in twelve-hour shifts. (It wasn't how I thought marriage would be!) Since I couldn't tolerate smoking or drinking during that first pregnancy, I ate tons of food. After seven months, I had gained all the weight my doctor would allow. He put me on the Weight Watchers program, and I had to be weighed once a week. I developed huge stretch marks. (There went bikinis and smooth skin!)

After my first son was born, I went back to smoking cigarettes, drinking, and partying. I also used speed, LSD, and pot. My husband was drinking all this time, and we moved several times. Soon I was pregnant with my second son. Getting pregnant seemed like a way of starting over—but my problems always followed!

In my early twenties, I saw the movie *Jesus Christ Superstar*. I wept afterward because I realized that I "believed" again. After seeing this movie, I felt totally forgiven for all the things I had done wrong. My husband and I joined a church, and I prayed with the pastor's wife that I could stop getting drunk. It didn't work, and I soon lost my faith.

We had our third son. When he was three months old, our in-laws bought a resort and invited us to help them run it. They hoped to get my husband away from his current job so that he would stop using speed. With the combination of booze and speed, he was becoming scary to be with at times.

We agreed to help them and, for a second time, lived with our in-laws. My husband, my father-in-law, and I were all drinking, leaving my mother-in-law to deal with us. I got very depressed: I couldn't even keep *my* apartment clean, and now I had to clean *other* people's rooms. The town had only five hundred people and I felt they judged us. My self-esteem was very low. I missed my friends and family.

One day I joined a women's bowling league—and the members were drinkers! I loved it! In fact, it got so that all I looked forward to was that one night out! I promptly experienced my first blackout and then acted in a way I wasn't proud of. During the next three years, I blacked out every time I drank. There were times I drove into ditches, didn't remember driving home, or couldn't recall what I had done for whole evenings. Finally, I was almost raped. That was my bottom.

For seven weeks, I went to AA meetings and stayed sober, even though I was working in a bar full-time (to me, this was a miracle). By the sixth week, I'd begun to get depressed again. I talked to Bill about my going to treatment but he flatly refused. I went to my boss, and he said that alcoholism was all in a person's head and that you just had to "make up your mind." So I prayed: "God, if you're there, then you're going to have to help me, because I've done everything I know how." I felt very guilty, and my life looked bleak. I drank two more times. Finally, half-drunk and sick, I drove thirty miles to the town where my counselor had her office and then had her drive me another two hours to treatment. God truly had answered my prayer!

My husband didn't support my going into treatment; he even threatened to divorce me. He thought it was the straw that broke the camel's back. I felt like we were strangers.

In treatment I learned to laugh again, and I *loved* having people to talk to. When I left treatment, I felt a glimmer of hope that maybe I could change. Six months later, I confronted my husband about *his* drinking; although very angry, he went into treatment.

Those were tough years. I was trying to find out who I was, be a mother, learn to be assertive, and attend a lot of meetings. My husband, still angry about my previous drinking behavior, was often sarcastic.

With one year of sobriety, I got a job as a unit assistant at a chemical dependency inpatient treatment center. My heart was really in my work. But six months later, my in-laws came to live with us (together again for the *third* time), and I got depressed and wanted to drink. I ended up going into therapy for a while, and that was very helpful. Going to AA and having a sponsor through the years have been my greatest helps.

Now that my drinking was manageable, food became an issue again. For the first three years of my sobriety, I did not diet. I feel God gave me the grace to let go of the food issue because staying sober was so difficult. But then I went on an eight-hundred-calorie diet with a friend—and it was so easy. I thought I'd just lose a few pounds. Instead, I became obsessed with getting thinner. No loss of weight was enough; I still felt fat. I had heard about bulimia and since I was used to vomiting (due to nausea), I tried vomiting a few times when I thought I had eaten too much. It worked—but then I couldn't stop.

Mt therapist suggested I go to Overeaters Anonymous. I went three times, but each time I got a headache. I decided against OA and instead went to the university hospital for outpatient treatment for my eating disorder. There I mainly learned about good nutrition (and vomited only once during that eight-week program). Afterward, I started acting bulimic again. I was simply not ready!

But my Higher Power had another plan for me. One day, my best friend called and invited me to an open OA meeting. Before I knew it, I had said yes and she'd hung up. I went, listened to the speakers, but decided it was too hard and that I still wasn't ready. Then my friend told me that our relationship was over, because she couldn't watch me binge and purge any more. I cried all the way home from the meeting. Once again I surrendered to God and said, "Okay, God, take the sugar! But I won't have anything to go to and my marriage will fall apart."

So began my journey into recovery with OA. Working the OA program has allowed me to stop beating up on myself over how much I weigh, over how much I've eaten, over diet after diet, and over vomiting. In OA, I have truly come to know myself.

Through OA, I've learned to be more of a partner to my husband. Our marriage nearly broke up after my first two years in OA, because I was getting clear on some sexuality issues and realizing when I was angry. But we came through the storm and celebrated.

With the help of God and the support of family, friends, and Twelve Step programs, I've now faced alcoholism, smoking, and bulimia/compulsive overeating. But the last two years have actually been the hardest.

In all these years of recovery, my goal has been to ensure my mental health. My greatest fear was that I would end up like my schizophrenic mother. I've always been a somewhat moody person, with periods of depression—not unlike most people, I thought. I would be really busy for a while, and then after a few days or a week, I would crash. I'd cry on my bed and feel I could not give—or even talk—to one more person. That mood might last a day, and then I would gear up again.

But about two years ago, several stressful things all happened around the same time. In therapy, I started talking about childhood issues. At work I had a two-week stretch where I put in nearly eighty hours (and then went home and spent four or five hours after work on my hobby, making recovery dolls—I felt so creative!). I crashed and got low. I didn't feel good again except for perhaps one week out of a month. I thought it was PMS. Soon each day was a great effort. I went to the doctor and had blood tests. The doctor could find nothing physical. I was referred to a therapist. As I described my up times and down times, the therapist decided I needed to see a psychiatrist. That scared me.

I went to the psychiatrist and, for the first time, heard about cyclothymia. Since there has been a lot of depression and manic-depressive illness in my family, he suggested I take an antidepressant. I felt the effect right away. (For some reason I didn't mind taking an antidepressant, but I didn't ever want to take lithium!) I then had about a three-month period where I felt very uninhibited and sexual. It was great!

Before antidepressants, I would feel great for short periods—but neither my husband nor I could figure out what had triggered it. During those times, I almost felt possessed—it was so unlike me! Now I see they were manic episodes. Eventually, I felt too much quivering energy inside, so in order to be myself again, I went off the antidepressant.

For the last year, I have gone on and off medication, not wanting to believe that I was powerless over these mood swings. I tried to work the program, to do all the things I knew how to do in order to function. I was able to do my job for quite a while (although I kept dropping shifts). But finally, I couldn't tolerate it any longer. I quit my job of twelve years. My self-esteem, how I saw myself on the job, was worse than how others saw me.

The difference these days is that I can't seem to pull it all together. I keep falling apart. In the past year, I've had to leave work three times and leave my OA meeting twice. I started to have that quivering feeling again, and so I went off medication, thinking that was the cause. No such luck. The quivering got worse. It got so I couldn't sleep much. In pain, I went back to eating sugar products and gained weight for the first time since coming to OA.

I was getting scared about the quivering feeling; I worried that it was memories coming up or even something "evil." I asked people from my church to pray for me. My moods went up and down over a twenty-four-hour period. I was unpredictable, and it was very difficult for my family. Finally, I went back to the doctor. Defeated, I went on lithium. I tried it for one month, but I felt tired all the time (and also missed the up times); so I took a lower dose. My moods quit fluctuating. Recently I also went on a low dose of a different type of antidepressant. This combination of lithium and antidepressant has brought back my sanity and the "real" me.

The thing that bothered me most over these past two years was that my life had finally become good. My marriage was better than ever, my children were almost grown, and I was in solid recovery. It made no sense that I was having such problems.

I've been back at work now for a couple of months, and I believe again in my ability to do my job and do it well. I'm good at it! I feel my feet are firmly planted; I feel strong in my abstinence, my sobriety, my ability to work, and my faith in God and in who I am—a beautiful woman in her forties who has a bipolar disorder.

ERIC'S STORY

I WAS TWENTY-THREE YEARS OLD when agoraphobia deposited me into a black hole of terror, fragility, and frustration.

As a boy, I was terrified of the uncertain elements around me. My parents drank constantly and used violence as a means of punishment. As a child, I needed attention and love, craved a smile or friendly word. My home life was a constant battleground of angry words and fists. Keeping to myself and staying out of the way of conflict was the only way to survive. Just keeping my mouth shut was the best way to avoid an angry word or a beating. I was a bed wetter until I was thirteen years old; I had painful headaches daily and couldn't read until I was seven. As an "imperfect child," I never felt worthy; I always wanted to be twenty years older. To me, childhood was only for kids.

At the age of fifteen, struggling with doubts about my sexuality, I escaped a home of terror through my twenty-three-year-old girlfriend. The doubts about my heterosexuality caught up with me, though, and I began a life of gay prostitution and alcohol and drug abuse at seventeen. I thought that in this lifestyle, I had finally found a way out of my fears, tears, and doubts. My life was spent avoiding my true self through sex, alcohol, and drugs. It was a wonderful life of irresponsibility, control, and adventure. The hidden, scared little boy was finally gone. I had washed his memory away. Abusing chemicals helped me to find the control I so desperately felt I needed. I could be any person I wanted to be. But I was constantly in trouble with the law for alcohol-related incidents. I would get out of jail and then do more of the same. I was on an endless journey, looking for love and companionship anywhere I could find them. As long as I kept up the binges of alcohol, sex, and drugs, fear never entered my mind. But I had locked up this powerful emotion within me for too long, and I knew that it would raise its ugly head eventually.

That day came when I was twenty-three years old.

I had quit drinking the year before: A DUI had scared me into realizing that alcohol could be a problem for me. I didn't, however, believe I needed treatment for alcoholism. Needing any kind of help was a sign of weakness—a sign that I wasn't in control, and I demanded that I always be in control.

So I continued doing drugs and thinking that alcohol was my only problem.

One evening, after doing about three days' worth of drugs, I experienced my first panic attack. It felt like doom. I was sure that I was going to die. My heart was palpitating, and it was almost impossible to breathe. I thought the world was collapsing and that I was going to collapse with it. The next day I drove to the beach, blamed the episode on bad drugs, and put my night of fear completely out of my thoughts.

Over the next three weeks, still taking my drugs as usual, I again experienced the attacks of terror, the heart palpitations, and the urge to run away, but again I refused to listen to my body. I was sure I was getting bad drugs, but I couldn't sit by myself without being high. The world was too quiet; I needed noise to cover up the feelings of extreme loneliness.

Around this time I was diagnosed HIV-positive, and my world went black. I felt I had no life left. I was sure that I was going to die before I was thirty. I hated myself for being gay, and I hated my parents for having a gay son. I didn't care about myself or anyone around me. I needed desperately to run from the pain and fear. Eventually my body and mind couldn't take it anymore.

One night while lying in bed, very high on cocaine, I disappeared. My sight went black. I felt great pain, as if someone had taken a hot iron rod and run it through me, from my toes to the last strand of hair on my head. I was sure I was dying.

For eight hours, I lay on my bed, unable to move for fear of the heart palpitations. Each time I tried to get out of bed, my heart would beat as if I were running a marathon. The panic attacks had begun to control me. I was housebound.

Over the next few years, I tried to find relief in self-help books, doctors, friends, and anyone who would listen to my crazy stories. I was sure that I would have to live my life as a prisoner of my own mind.

After three years, it all got to be too much, and I tried to find relief again in alcohol and drugs. My panic attacks promptly disappeared, and I was overjoyed. But my joy was short-lived. After just two weeks of self-medication with alcohol and drugs, my panic attacks returned one hundredfold. No matter how much alcohol I drank, no matter how much cocaine I snorted, it was not enough: The panic was knocking on my door, saying, "I haven't left yet."

After three months with no relief, the panic had become so debilitating that I couldn't bathe or dress myself. The living room became my bed. I couldn't move; I couldn't speak. Fear had won.

It was only then that I went into treatment for my alcoholism.

Today I have been in recovery for twenty-two months. The panic attacks come and go on a pretty regular basis. When I stray in my recovery process, I know that the attacks get worse. I know that alcohol isn't the answer—it's the enemy—and that my problems only get worse when I medicate my world with chemicals. I still suffer from daily anticipatory anxiety, but it doesn't scare me as much and I still have a lot of work to do. I know today that I can't run the show, that I need people. And that's okay.

Phobics Anonymous has taught me that I'm not alone with my fears anymore. There are people to talk to about what is going on with me, people I know have been there before me. Just being able to open my mouth and talk about Eric is a wonderful gift. I have learned that it's okay to be me, an imperfect human being.

GENNA'S STORY

FOR ALMOST a decade, I worked hard to make my life miserable. Diagnosed with anorexia nervosa at nineteen, I struggled first with anorexia, then bulimia, and finally with depression. Ultimately, after years of fighting against myself and with the world around me, I began to recover from my dual disorder by working the Twelve Step program.

I became anorexic during my senior year in high school. The oldest child in a highly intelligent, competitive family, I was simply overwhelmed with anxiety about proving myself in college. Becoming anorexic was a good way to avoid proving anything other than that I could be thinner than anyone else. My family members watched my deterioration in silence. My mother worked full-time and had been our only parent since my alcoholic father left us when I was four. My sister appeared isolated from the family, secure in her world of high school friends, and my brother escaped by attending a private boarding school on a scholarship.

During my four years at college, my life revolved around my body and food. While I received many academic honors and earned grades that landed me in the top 10 percent of my class, I didn't mark progress by what appeared on my transcript. Instead, I measured the merit of my life by the numbers on a scale or the markings of a tape measure.

By my senior year in college, I didn't care enough about anything other than sustaining my illness. I had systematically isolated myself from the people who cared about me. My friends were exhausted from four years of trying to help me and receiving only hostility for their efforts. I had minimal contact with my family and had finally cut myself off from them altogether when my mother demanded that I go into treatment.

While other college seniors were out looking for jobs, I occupied myself with keeping my weight below seventy-five pounds. This took up any time I might have had for extra homework, job searches, or friendships. All I could think about was food and the bones of my body.

I set my alarm for 3 A.M. every day. Taking a jump rope with me, I crept through the sleeping dorm hallways to the women's shower. The empty room was dimly lit, cold, and gray in the middle of the night, and I would jump rope for forty minutes on the cracking concrete. After returning to bed for a couple of hours, I would get up at 5:30 or 6 A.M. to jog. The rest of my day was usually spent studying—and fighting off the urge to eat—in the library. I brought potato chips or candy into the library with me, occasionally giving in to my hunger and then running to the bathroom to vomit.

Occasionally I would binge and vomit. More often than not, I stole money to fund these food frenzies. Once, I stole my roommate's money and some of our belongings to make it look as if someone had broken into our dorm room. If one of my friends took me out to dinner (as people were prone to do, trying to "help" me eat), I would eat what most people would call a normal meal and then throw it up when I returned to my dorm. This satisfied my need to please the people around me by feigning some sort of motion toward recovery. But it was an act. I considered any amount of food, other than a handful of carrots or an apple, to be a binge. So every time I ate "normally" in public, I vomited as soon as I could.

Most of my friends watched in bewilderment as my illness escalated. One told me, with much love and sadness, that she could no longer be around me. She couldn't stand by and watch my self-destruction. Slowly, many of my friends drifted away.

Ultimately, after years of starvation and abuse, it was my own body that demanded I seek treatment. I fainted after my daily morning jog. When I woke, I found myself in a hospital emergency room, surrounded by blinking red lights, plastic tubes, and people in white lab coats. The emergency room staff convinced me that my life was in danger. If I wanted to live, I would need to go into treatment for anorexia.

I did. My hospital stay lasted a little over a year. Initially, I was eager to recover, simply because I wanted to live. However, when I saw that recovery entailed not only gaining weight (which was bad enough), but changing fundamental beliefs I held about myself, I began resisting recovery and fighting the hospital staff as fiercely as I had fought my family and friends.

Going through the motions of treatment, I began drinking water and diet soda to boost my weight. I taped scissors and padlocks around my chest before I was weighed. Soon I was vomiting whatever I ate into garbage cans, plastic bags—whatever I could find. Every time there was an opportunity to sneak off the hospital ward to binge and vomit, I seized it.

My life revolved around tricking the people trying to help me. It seemed so easy, almost like a game.

But the stakes skyrocketed suddenly. I ripped a small hole in my esophagus trying to choke out the single apple I had eaten earlier. Long shots of pain tore through my throat and began spreading throughout my back. I knew something was terribly wrong, and I went back to the eating disorder ward. The staff rushed me to surgery.

The surgeon informed me that I had about a 50 percent chance of living. The rip in my esophagus was allowing air to spread throughout the interior of my body, seeping into places air didn't belong. The pain was incredible. The surgeon was reluctant to operate because my potassium level and electrolytes were dangerously low from vomiting.

I had to make a decision—take my chances with surgery or hope that the hole in my throat would heal itself spontaneously before the air seepage did permanent damage. With the surgeon's advice, I chose the second option. I spent a week with an IV in my arm, staying in the surgery unit in case the hole didn't close by itself and the doctors would be forced to perform emergency surgery.

The rip in my esophagus did begin to close. It was a slow, painful process. My body ached. My throat was so fragile and sore that I couldn't even swallow water. Any movement was discouraged as it could jar open the slowly healing hole. I felt trapped, utterly hopeless and abandoned. There were no friends left to visit me. My mother refused to come and see me, saying she'd had enough. Every day, the doctors who came into my room told me that I was lucky to be alive.

The possibility of death suddenly became real to me. This became a turning point in my illness. Sometime during those long hours I spent alone, I decided to begin fighting *for* my life instead of against it. Not only did that mean a physical recovery, I realized, but a psychological and spiritual one as well. Having nowhere else to go, I asked God for help. Even while I was talking to "Him," I didn't quite know what I meant by "God," but I knew that I needed something stronger than myself. For the first time in my life, I acknowledged my own weakness, my own powerlessness.

When my physical strength returned, I left the hospital determined to find a way to end the chaos and despair that had taken over my life. It was important to me to begin my recovery in a new place, with new people who would help me heal psychically, as well as physically. I spent almost two months interviewing therapists and visiting treatment centers.

Eventually, I began therapy with a woman at a social service agency. My relationship with Beth lasted almost three years. For the first time, I was committed to my recovery and eager to get on with the business of living. In addition to my individual therapy with Beth, I began attending Bulimics/Anorexics Anonymous (BAA) meetings.

I had learned about the Twelve Step program in the hospital but only now began to really understand and use it. Instead of studying the Steps, I lived them. Still unsure about the word *God*, I let my BAA group and Beth become my Higher Power. I worked hard in therapy, digging into the corners of my life and investigating every incident, every emotion I found there. My responsibility as a member of a community became important to me; I took pride in participating in my BAA group as completely and authentically as possible. During this time, I gained weight, my eating habits stabilized, and I began developing strong friendships. I had many difficult moments, but I was able to survive them by turning to my BAA group for guidance. I also had moments of great joy, times when I was overwhelmed with the beauty of the world around me and the people in it.

Once out of therapy, I continued my recovery on my own. My circle of friends continued to grow, and I started identifying myself in ways other than "anorexic." I began graduate school. Soon I had a strong group of friends, a supportive lover, and a promising academic career. I read everything I could get my hands on regarding codependency, recovery, eating disorders, and spirituality. In many ways, I was starting my life from scratch, rejecting the religion I was raised in and the behavior patterns that I had established over the years of my illness. More than anything else, I enjoyed this process of rebuilding and discovery.

Yet, after more than a year of this new life, I began to be overcome by periods of exhaustion. I didn't feel strong, as I had during the early stages of my recovery. Getting out of bed in the mornings became difficult; I never felt entirely awake or rested. It seemed that I always needed just a little more sleep, no matter how much I had slept the night before. Eventually, sleep became impossible to control. I began falling asleep in the library, on buses, during classes.

I slowly became too tired to care about maintaining my recovery. There was no energy to call a friend when I felt like skipping a meal or to challenge my own thinking when I decided to lose a few pounds. While my work as a graduate student had brought me opportunities and rewards, I was too tired to follow up on anything, to take the next steps in my career. My weight dropped. I stopped caring about everything that I had worked so hard for.

But something inside of me was still strong enough to make me seek counseling again. This time, the therapist at the university I was attending concluded that my primary problem at this moment was depression. The depression drained me of the energy I needed to sustain my recovery from anorexia. The return of my anorexic thoughts and behaviors added to my depression. The therapist prescribed an antidepressant.

Although I had told myself that I would do anything to feel energetic and happy again, I was reluctant to take the medication. Intellectually, I understood and agreed with everything the therapist told me. Depression even ran in our family. My mother had taken antidepressants for years; my sister began taking them after a nearly successful suicide attempt. I had seen the symptoms of depression in my mother and sister and now saw them in myself. When other people took prescription medicine, I saw it as the intelligent, healthy thing to do. When faced with filling my own prescription for antidepressants, I saw it as a sign of failure and weakness.

My therapist patiently helped me work through this resistance. She supplied literature about depression and recounted stories of people she knew who had turned their lives around when they began taking appropriate medication. Slowly, I realized that I couldn't simply *will* myself out of what I had been calling a "slump." Depression was a medical problem that required medication. Just as I had trusted my BAA group and Beth to guide me when my own vision failed, I decided to trust this new therapist and begin taking the medication.

The fog I had been living under lifted eventually. As I began feeling more hopeful and energetic, I began entering into a new level of my recovery. The depression ultimately forced me to reassess the course I had mapped for my recovery. I was able to identify some destructive patterns and unhealthy relationships that had re-emerged in my life. I was also better able to see and appreciate all of the progress I had made, the stable relationships that I had developed.

More importantly, I confronted a fact that I had been vaguely aware of and reluctant to face: During my depression, I had become so apathetic that some of my old eating patterns had surfaced. With the help of my medication, I had the energy to again ask for the help I needed with my eating disorder. With the love, support, and patience of my friends and BAA group, I was able to restabilize my eating and my weight.

Finally, during this time I was given an important spiritual gift. After years of struggling to define "God" through reading about spirituality and religion, I threw aside my books and simply looked at the world around me. Giving up my resistance to the antidepressant had somehow pushed me the distance I needed to go in order to abandon the intellectual control I maintained over my "spirituality" and to experience my spirit instead. Without books to read or theories to test, I began understanding spirituality through the experiences of my own life and through my relationships with other people.

Today my life is infinitely more complex—and simple—than I had ever imagined it could be. Life is simple in that it exists only one day at a time for me. Each day, I do what is essential. I take one green and white pill, feed my body, and treat myself and the people around me with love, respect, and compassion. These are the basics.

The complexities stem from all of this. I have discovered hundreds of things I enjoy doing—from writing, reading, and painting, to sailing, swimming, and biking. I have friends I love deeply and whose lives have been intimate parts of my own. My work is going well, and each day I make progress toward completing my Ph.D. Every day is rich, full of small and large pleasures.

I can manage and enjoy the complexities of my life because they are all extras. Underneath the books, the friends, the academic projects, and camping trips are the basics: taking my medication, eating well, and respecting life—my own and other people's. This foundation provides the base of ethics and health in my life. The two are not unrelated.

Jay's Story

T HE PLACE TO start is with the amazing fact that I've lived to be forty years old. The only explanation is that there is a God and that Twelve Step recovery programs and therapy are lethal weapons against dying moment by moment. And if people work really hard at it, they can get all the way to One Whole Day at a Time.

I stopped drinking and using at twenty-four—for me, that was the easy part. I went to meetings, got a sponsor, and did what I was told most of the time. The problem was that my hair was past my shoulders, my favorite black T-shirt read "Kill 'Em All and Let God Sort 'Em Out," I wore my dark glasses all the time (even in meetings), and I was six feet six inches and weighed 235 pounds. *Nobody* (not even suicidal people) would confront my antisocial behavior in any Twelve Step meetings.

I remained this way for eight years. At the time, it wasn't obvious to me that anything was wrong. I had made some changes—bought some nice suits, gotten a job as a salesman—and, surprisingly, did well for a while, "acting" socially acceptable.

Then I met my wife-to-be. (We're still married. I am amazed and extremely grateful.) Seven years ago, we said our "I do's." She had a steady job, but about a week before our wedding, I became unemployed.

I then began to isolate myself; I started reacting to everything she said and did—at times grabbing her, yelling and cussing at her, throwing things. I felt like a wolf caught in a trap. (My wife is only five feet two inches tall, and she's pleasant unless provoked.) I became cold, distant, and volatile.

By the time we'd been married about three months, I'd gone through two jobs because of my behavior at work. One place even accused me of being "drunk." (Not so—it's just that an antisocial personality looks that way to "regular" people.) At this point, my wife suggested treatment, and since I had never been to treatment, I knew this was a "communist plot"—after all, I'd been sober four years longer than she! "She's sick" is what I heard from my sponsor and four other people who knew us in the fellowship. So I continued with meetings and continued to be antisocial and blame the rest of the world. I had lots of enablers within the programs, both AA and NA.

Three more months went by. By this time, I was on my fourth job. With six years of college and a B.A. in psychology, I was working in a warehouse. I worked alone, which was comfortable, except that the loneliness was killing me.

Late one Friday morning, finally in tears, I called a friend who worked in the addictions field. "I'm losing it," I said. He came and picked me up, and we called a treatment center. For me it was either a state hospital, a rubber room, or suicide. (I knew enough not to verbalize the last option, or it would definitely have been the rubber room.) The treatment center said it could take me on Sunday. I stopped back by work and told my co-workers where I was going. I was petrified I wouldn't have a job. I was grateful to be working again, but I thought I was also being used (that was part of my problem).

I went through the twenty-eight days, and thank God I got a therapist who was bigger than me and could communicate with the antisocial part of me. He suggested that I wouldn't know a feeling if it bit me! He asked me how I felt. My response was full of anger, hatred, and rage. He began to teach me about my antisocial reactions to my feelings. And he began to teach me what was going on below the antisocial behavior—the sadness, loneliness, insecurity, and inadequacy; the terrified, hurt, trapped, used, unloved, unaccepted, and shameful feelings. I soon realized that I had learned three rules growing up in my home, on the streets, and in my culture: Don't Talk, Don't Trust, Don't Feel. I especially learned Don't Feel, because feeling produces nothing and wastes time. After all, big boys don't cry (feel), do they?

When I got home after treatment, I was worried about being unemployed. But I was amazed when two treatment centers called and wanted me to do marketing and public relations for them. I took one of the positions. Within ninety days, another facility contacted me about becoming a therapist there. I took that job and have been doing therapy ever since (both for others and for myself).

Five years ago, I was given an opportunity to develop a codependency program. In order to do so I participated in a similar program as a patient/clinical observer and was introduced to the concept of the "child within."

This program involved a lot of "anger work," where you take an "encounter bat," scream at the top of your lungs, and beat the hell out of something. Then you hug your "child within," being kind and caring and loving toward that part of yourself. (Developmentally, this "child" falls in the age range of zero to eight years old.)

When I started to develop my own program, I began to run into snags—not only with other people (and with negative double messages that therapists and co-therapists and administrative people give), but with my own antisocial behaviors. They began to show up all over, which terrified me. So I reviewed all the work I had done thus far. Self-doubt—about my abilities, about life, and about people—ran through me. I spent nights at home wanting to quit my job, get divorced, and blame the world because I was still feeling the antisocial reactions in full force.

So I got into therapy on my own. (Therapy's not bad stuff, it's another tool. Bill W. spent a lot of time in therapy.) I believe that personality disorders and other psychiatric problems—which, contrary to some popular beliefs, alcoholics and addicts do have—require attention above and beyond the Twelve Steps. But I didn't know what I was looking for. I just knew things weren't complete and that it was a struggle to operate within the framework of socially acceptable behavior and keep a job.

By this time my attitude had changed to "Stay low and keep movin'." At work people referred to me as "unprofessional" and "crazy," but I had developed a reputation as a damn good therapist. The only person who would say much to me about my behavior was my co-therapist. Nobody else would confront me for fear of my reaction: I would win by intimidation. I'd intimidate people with a look I had developed out of fear as a kid on the streets—your basic psychopathic glare!

One day my co-therapist and I were discussing how we could make our codependency program more effective when she asked, "What are you going to do about the adolescent in you?" I replied, "What the hell are you talking about?"

But I calmed down, and we kept on talking. After a while, the personal part of her message became clear to me. We had been looking at the developmental age range of zero to eight years as constituting the years of the child within, but why couldn't there be a second developmental age range, say from nine to twenty-one or twenty-five years? We could call it the "adolescent within," who is rebellious and very antisocial. We agreed that it fit our model, and, more important, it fit me personally.

I continued with individual therapy, and one evening my therapist did a guided imagery exercise with me. Instead of meeting my child and taking him back to where he grew up, we took my *adolescent* back. He was seventeen years old, six feet six inches tall, 235 pounds, wearing his leathers, and riding a Harley Sportster. When he arrived at the house where he grew up, he saw that it had been burned down! Everything was gone—Mom, Dad, hopes, dreams, ambitions, wishes, everything! He walked into the middle of the charred rubble, sat down, and began to sob uncontrollably!

I remember that the pain and sadness were beyond anything I had ever experienced before. Death would have been easier to accept. Depression set in. It was real and it was devastating! Life felt like swimming in molasses. I could no longer run, and, most terrifying, I felt I could no longer fight.

But in working through this depression with my therapist, two things happened. First, I began to develop a broader understanding of Step Seven through the book *Twelve Steps and Twelve Traditions*. It talks about how once we get a handle on how *not* to drink, we will want to heave a great sigh of relief and say, "Well, thank God that's over." *Twelve and Twelve* goes on to say that we've only gotten to the first milestone and that in order not to relapse, it becomes critical to go back and find out what caused us to become "problem drinkers" (pre-alcoholic) in the first place.

Second, my therapist referred me to a psychiatrist who specializes in people who are chemically dependent. (Know that you have an obligation and a right to check these caregivers out thoroughly.) After several visits with both my therapist and psychiatrist and after extensive psychological testing, I was given a prescription for antidepressant medication.

I was (and am) very cautious about medication: It can be life-threatening but also life-saving. But I trust my therapist, who trusts my psychiatrist—a doctor I literally trust with my life.

I took antidepressants for about seven months. For most of this time, I worked on a ranch (the facility I'd worked for had just closed), rested, worked on myself, spent time with other therapists, and spent time in Twelve Step meetings.

During all this, my wife chose to go through it with me. (I can't thank her enough for the support!) I know there were a lot of days when she asked herself, *Why?* And I often asked myself that same question: There were many times I wanted to kill myself.

The other important part of my story began when I got tired of people telling me to read page 449 in the Big Book. (For example, "Unless I accept life completely on life's terms, I cannot be happy. I need to concentrate not so much on what needs to be changed in the world as on what needs to be changed in me and in my attitudes" and "I was always able to see the flaw in every person, every situation. And I was always glad to point it out. . . .") I had an antisocial reaction to the smart asses who'd say this; I wanted to jack them up against a wall, rip out page 449, and make them eat it. That would demonstrate how *acceptance* as the answer was not so fun or simple. (Their intentions were pure, I'm sure, but incomplete.)

Fortunately for all, I have grown beyond acting out these fantasies, and I don't even say them out loud much anymore. What I have finally realized after much research is this: "Acceptance is the answer to *all* my problems today."* But to get to acceptance, I first must go through shock, denial, anger, bargaining, and withdrawal/depression. In other words, I must go through the grief process (which happens any time there is a change in a person's life, no matter how big or small, whether positive or negative). I also need to accurately identify and experience my feelings. And if I cry, it's only natural. To lash out or react angrily is to misrepresent what's really going on; in fact, it's a lie, and the feelings remain stuffed and the issues unresolved.

To summarize, I have discovered this: My antisocial personality can be arrested (no pun intended) and held in check with a combination of approaches.

Doing Steps Four through Nine. In Step Four, I learn to accurately identify and experience my feelings. In Step Five, I take a risk and admit to God, myself, and another human being the *exact nature* of my wrongs; here I *react to* my feelings rather than accurately identifying and experiencing them. In Step Six, I become willing to have God remove all these defects of character. In Step Seven, I allow myself to go back and identify my self-defeating, antisocial behavioral patterns; in Steps Eight and Nine, I make amends for those patterns.

---

*Alcoholics Anonymous, 449.

Working Steps Ten, Eleven, and Twelve. These three steps allow me to avoid a buildup of garbage from the discoveries I've made and from the changes and grief I've gone through.

Using therapy. It continues to help me with reality checks, because I still need assistance in working within the framework of socially acceptable behavior.

Trusting my psychiatrist. (Over time, he's impressed me.) After much discussion—it was frightening when he suggested it—he placed me on lithium as a reaction stabilizer. The medication gives me the few extra seconds I need to hear the other person all the way through, to accurately identify what I'm feeling, and to respond in a socially acceptable manner. Otherwise I'd be a slave, *reacting* to my feelings with antisocial behaviors that ruin my life. (On the other hand, I have used alcohol and other drugs, food, or some other compulsive behavior to stuff my feelings. I believe that stuffing my feelings is the essence of my illness.)

I've found the best specialists I can; I talk to them about my symptoms, I let them know how I feel about what *we* are doing, and I follow their recommendations to the letter.

I know today that I deserve to *live*—maybe not happily ever after, but with as much balance as I can achieve on any given day at any given moment.

I am also genuinely grateful that I am able to have a reasonably balanced relationship with my wife, stepchildren, and grandson. Today I can be a part of their lives, sharing both joy and sorrow, rather than isolating and experiencing nothing.

JODY'S STORY

I AM THE SECOND in a family of six children. My parents moved to Minnesota when I was five years old, and I grew up in a small town, secure, comfortable, and filled with enthusiasm for school and play. Although my father was a surgeon, he paid a great deal of attention to his family; both of my parents focused their lives on us kids to the extent that we felt able to accomplish anything we chose to do.

As a result, I was always a high achiever, getting top grades and excelling in athletics. I also pursued my interest in writing and the arts from a young age. My interests didn't keep me from having friends. Home served as a gathering place for boys and girls, since my brothers and sisters and I came so close together in age.

I don't remember alcohol playing an important—or any— part in my family's lives until late in my teens. But when seemingly out of the blue, alcoholism had descended upon our family like a plague, my father admitted that his father had been a binge drinker.

When I drank for the first time, I was sixteen and having an innocent slumber party at my parents' lake cabin when they were out of town. Several girlfriends and I decided that it would be adventurous to break into my parents' liquor cabinet. We were all "good girls," the top students, the popular all-around leaders.

That night, I made a fool of myself, emptying the vodka and scotch and everything else completely and proclaiming to my girlfriends my undying love for a boy in our class. The boy I liked was disgusted when he heard about the incident; my father reprimanded me for raiding the liquor cabinet. For a week I vomited daily. I lost ten pounds. The boys noticed me as they never had before.

I went on to become one of the first women in the state to play on a varsity boys' team; I graduated from high school as valedictorian; and I was accepted at Yale University, one of the first women to enter as undergraduates. These achievements both exhilarated and depressed me.

The depression I experienced the spring of my senior year was, in fact, a clinical depression. I changed from a young woman interested in life to an irritable, argumentative, spoiled woman. I succeeded in alienating my childhood friends. One of my boyfriends bluntly told me that I needed to see a psychiatrist—I was clinging to him like a life raft. When he broke up with me, I felt like killing myself.

On my graduation night, I drank for the second time in my life, downing everything in sight until my other boyfriend (who hadn't abandoned me) ended up carrying me home over his shoulder. I was incapable of drinking moderately. I also displayed an excited manner close to mania.

I was leaving one world that I knew and loved for another, foreign world, the first big loss I would know. But I kept my gaze forward. The alcoholic bouts and the depression abated. I seemed to have a natural resilience and a great determination, or so I thought.

It takes great loss or a great stress to first trigger the disease known as manic-depression. Already I had experienced the depressive side of the illness, and in my first semester at Yale, I went into a manic phase that took on its own momentum.

My first semester at Yale I managed A's in advanced courses, became the first person in my class to write for the college newspaper, and made the women's varsity tennis team. My roommates were annoyed when I would jump out of the top bunk at 5 A.M., raring to go. Eventually the wound-up energy that I was exhibiting began to spin me out of control. For the first time, I started to "go in all directions," as I later learned to call it. By November, I found myself losing things; I locked myself out of my room constantly. I became hypersensitive and overanalyzed casual remarks.

Eventually, after a relaxing Christmas break in my hometown, I slowed down, which took the edge off the adjustment to Yale. Little did I suspect that I had triggered a deadly disease that now could rule my life in times of stress and that would progressively worsen in its manifestations. Changes in my brain chemistry had been set off by the pressure I had encountered. Just as with a case of heart disease, it becomes easier to set off this chemical imbalance each time a certain amount of stress is encountered.

I drank alcohol only once during my first semester at school, and that was close to the Christmas vacation. Need I say that I drank exactly as I had drunk twice before? I was accompanied by new friends, all men. I drank them under the table, but then I vomited on their shoes and made a fool of myself. "I knew you were different," said one friend, "the first time I saw you drink."

Although I always became quite ill after these isolated bouts, I loved the feeling I got when drunk. The euphoria and total abandonment seemed to be a part of my soul. Drunken ecstasy, like sexual orgasm, seemed a way to escape the emotional pain of my breaking away from Minnesota and moving into a new life.

It was all or nothing in everything I did, and in the way I was. Even now, when I know that to drink is to court death, I can honestly say that reality is never quite enough—only nowadays I try to develop spiritually and consciously what mania and booze *manufactured* for me back then: a heightened awareness of the possibilities in life and people.

I discovered tequila with the graduating seniors that year, and by the end of my sophomore year, I was spending half of my time on campus at the bar where the rugby players hung out (my boyfriend played rugby). I also started a pattern that persisted until I finally became sober ten years later: All of my boyfriends were alcoholic.

My sexual activity during those years mirrored the trends I observed in most of my friends. In my circles, there was never much of a double standard concerning sex, and I don't feel guilty about the fact that I have slept with so many men. But I did violate the principle I had held as a young woman, which was that sex, if not marriage, was sacred. I know I lost some self-esteem by trying to have sex in the seemingly casual manner that men did (although I don't know many men who can *really* do that either).

I loved sex the way I loved getting drunk. Being admitted to a school that had only recently gone coed was like being let loose in a candy store. I retained enough of my Catholic inhibitions that it was difficult for me to sleep with men unless I was manic or drunk or both, but since I was always drunk, I took full advantage of the fact that there were a great many young men around with raging hormones, and very few women. On one day during my senior year, I slept with three men, one in the morning, one in the afternoon, and then my boyfriend later that night. After I told him what I had done that day, all he said was, "Do you still have your diaphragm in?"

Once I became so wound up over a school assignment, I went to the health center for advice and a staff member gave me Valium. I went back to my room and took the whole bottle. It wasn't a suicide attempt; I just knew that I needed that much to come down. I slept for a day and a half, got up, and went to dinner.

No one noticed that I appeared any different, which allowed me to think that I could handle these ups and downs on my own. I was conscious that something was wrong with me but I was even more self-conscious that I should appear "normal" to my classmates.

Another time, without being on any medication, I experienced a full-blown hallucination. It was different from any dream or imaginary visualization I had ever had. A three-dimensional phantom of a girl from another century appeared before my eyes. I shook myself completely awake, but I knew then that I had a powerful visual ability that could control me if I let it.

An indication of how my illness affected my life occurred one day when I casually told my boyfriend that I might kill myself someday. I didn't really mean it. I had been thinking about Virginia Woolf, my "heroine" at the time, and my boyfriend and I were walking by the ocean. He was very disturbed by this comment and sidestepped out of the relationship without further discussion. In one way or another, either my alcoholism or my bipolar disorder interfered with my romantic relationships.

Looking back now, I am able to accept these losses as being caused by illness, but at the time, such quick cuts in relationships hurt a great deal. Had I known then what I know now about dual disorders, I think I might have avoided breakups and had a different life altogether.

When college ended, I felt lost. I decided to go to New York City with my college roommate and break into book publishing. My drinking was already beginning to strain our friendship. When we arrived in New York, we realized that we had made too big a jump too fast. She left to live with her boyfriend, and I promptly got pregnant by a friend from Yale. I didn't want to get married (and neither did he), so I left New York after two months, returned to Minnesota, and had an abortion.

By the time I returned to Minnesota, everyone in my family had turned out to be alcoholic, which became clear the first time any of us drank. The whole family was veering toward disaster.

The two years I spent in Minneapolis are lost in a blur of booze and drugs. I found a group of graduate students who were into drugs of all kinds. Although I had never experimented with anything but alcohol before, I now found the pleasures of cocaine, acid, and mushrooms. Multi-drug nights became a norm on weekends, where everyone at parties ended up sleeping with everyone else. There seemed to be no limit to the decadence I would indulge in, and yet no one, I thought, could see this. I could still, anytime I cared to, put on the good-girl student act and get away with it.

During those years, my manic-depression was mostly in hiding, but cocaine would bring it out. I could lose twelve pounds in two days after doing one hit of cocaine, because coke would trigger a manic reaction. Coming down from these manias would drop me into a clinical depression, and sleeping around was taking its toll on my self-esteem.

After two years of living in Minnesota, taking one job after another, becoming involved with one man after another, making stabs at writing but never being very clearheaded about it, I found myself suicidally depressed. I was coming off a drug and booze binge and facing the fact that my primary lover had fallen in love with another woman, when one of my college friends called me from New York. He was being promoted, he said, and he thought I could get his old job as an assistant editor.

I got the job, but I lost myself. Within six months of arriving in New York City, I had what I thought I had always wanted. My literary talents received immediate recognition, and I discovered that I'd finally found a business I enjoyed and excelled at: book publishing. I had a lover, a talented editor, who drank as much as I did. For the first time in my adult life, I fell in love with someone who fell in love with me. We moved in together.

The fact that my lover was married didn't bother me. His wife had moved out of state. All of a sudden I had an instant family, with his two daughters visiting us and staying with us during summer vacations. I found that I enjoyed the role of "stepmother," and I was happy with my personal life. Work also continued to go well.

With my first attempt at writing a book proposal, I acquired an agent and got a book contract. A friend and I started a magazine and found ourselves being invited to the homes of famous writers.

While I had all the elements of a good life, my continued drinking began to change how I managed that life. My conflicts with other people intensified, and I began to lose friends. My lover and I were rowdy drunks, turning over tables in restaurants, getting thrown out of bars. But we also piled up creative success after creative success. Our only fights occurred when my mania "broke through" and the amount of alcohol I was consuming could not cover up these changes in mood. I would go overboard, throwing jealous fits about his wife, and finally throwing things around the apartment.

We separated for the first time the morning after I threw an ashtray through a window in a drunken rage and he put my head through a glass door. I went back to Minnesota. There I drank every day, but in Minnesota, a lower-key environment, the manic surges died down. My friends in Minnesota took one look at how I was drinking and called me an alcoholic. I laughed and told them about the wild times in New York City. My lover called and wrote constantly, and we agreed to get back together. So I flew back to New York City to move in with him and to find a new job.

The next year and a half were the most conventional years of my adult life. I was living with a man I loved, we both worked in the book publishing business, and we both were advancing in our careers. I loved my new job, and it remains the only job that I think of as a place where I could have made a life and found a career. But even with these outwardly acceptable trappings of tradition, incidents precipitated a blowup. We drank every day, but we had reached the same level of alcoholism together and functioned with it.

I recall that on some mornings, I'd stop behind buildings on the way to work and vomit. My lover and I would begin our weekends by each drinking a quart of hard liquor. Then we'd go out to dinners and to parties; several times he had to carry me home afterward. We had fights like the one that had broken us up, but they didn't become physically violent. The next day we'd walk through Riverside Park, and I'd beg him to tell me that he loved me. "I don't love that part of you," he'd say. The mania was beginning to take on its own personality, and he could see it.

One Sunday night, after drinking several martinis, I picked up the phone to call my lover's wife in New Mexico to demand that she sign the divorce papers. My lover took the phone away from me. I picked up a seltzer bottle and brought it down forcefully on his toe; he pushed me and I fell face forward, knocking my top teeth against the kitchen floor. That push, that fall, and the fragments of my teeth flying became a metaphor for my broken life.

When I left our home the next day, it was for the last time. My lover and I fought and saw one another, but we never again lived together.

So my office became my home in essence. It took me months to resettle in Manhattan, and I was happy neither with my new roommate nor with my physical surroundings. I spent as much time as possible in the office. It soon was apparent that I wasn't adjusting to the breakup of my relationship. After drinking every night, I could barely make it to work on time. I lost weight rapidly, dropping to a weight that I hadn't been since I was a kid. People said that I was acting like a child, that I had somehow regressed to an emotional age much younger than I was. But I kept going because I was manic, and manics have extraordinary stamina and energy. In fact, I barely slept. My head buzzed like a mosquito. I stalked my ex-lover, breaking in at our old home, interrupting his new relationship.

I knew I needed help. My boss agreed to let me take all the time off I wanted. I asked him if the company insurance covered inpatient treatment for alcoholism. He didn't know anything about the disease of alcoholism and said he thought I was drinking too much because of my relationship breakup. A true alcoholic, I immediately accepted this notion so I could excuse my own behavior.

Meaning well, my boss decided that I would be better off with a better-paying job elsewhere, since I had relied on my lover's income to live well in Manhattan. Had my boss had any inkling of the difficulties involved in being placed on the street in the midst of a manic-depressive/alcoholic breakdown, he wouldn't have done that to me.

My last months in New York City that year remain lost. I found one job after another and did well, despite the fact that I was drinking a bottle of wine for breakfast. I was offered a promotion at one job after a month—an indication of how manic brain activity can, if disciplined, actually help achievement, but I turned that job down to take another job at a publishing company. There I was canned within weeks for being "crazy"; the continued stress of job jumping had pushed the mania past the productive stage. I was talking off the top of my head to anyone I met. I spent hours at bars at night, and I often couldn't remember how I got home (when I did get home). I slept with dozens of strange men and would wake in parts of the city I didn't recognize. I had written an eight-page poem and would read it at bars. I kept getting thinner and thinner. I had no control over my drinking or the mania, and by the end, I was a walking, talking pathology.

It's extremely dangerous for a woman alone to take subways at 3 A.M. from Manhattan into Brooklyn; when I did so, I was deliberately taunting street gangs. The only reason I didn't get into more trouble is that people who live on the streets know when someone is nuts, and they leave that person alone. I was so boozed up that I was only half-conscious of my own actions; the full memory of these events returned to me later in flashbacks. It was like living in a dream, a nightmare. The manic activity, combined with the alcohol I was consuming daily, insulated me almost completely from the reality of the world in which I was living and the things I was doing. Because of this, I wasn't even suicidal; the real me, the conscious mind, was drowned in booze, and the mania was nearly full insanity, which for the only time in my life would become a psychotic break.

When the mania led to psychosis, I was staying overnight at the place of my new boyfriend, a friend of a college friend. I woke him up in the middle of the night. I was completely confused, neither in this world nor any other, mixing up books I had read with my own life. The next day I continued to behave strangely. My boyfriend called my father that day, who then called me and told me to take the next plane out of Manhattan. Had I not obeyed, there is no doubt in my mind that I would have ended up either hospitalized for a very long time or dead.

When my father called me, I came to some sense of the real danger of my situation. I continued to drink, but I did leave New York City. I have no memory of how I got to the airport, how I got on the plane, or anything that happened between his call and my arrival in Minneapolis. I'd left everything I owned at my place in Brooklyn.

When my mother greeted me, I spouted quotes from books I had read, completely disoriented. I was also very drunk. My parents immediately took me to a hospital, but I refused to see a doctor. It's quite common for those of us who have manic-depression to deny that we need help. I insisted on recuperating in my hometown, and my parents agreed. Given the trauma of the months I had endured in New York after breaking up with my lover and losing my job, returning to my hometown was my subconscious way of finding safety, of finding myself.

I blocked out most of the traumatic events in New York City and simply picked up my life in Minnesota. But denial characterizes both drinking and mania. I quickly felt physically fine, and I managed to find jobs in Minneapolis. But I kept on drinking for the next year and a half. I had run-ins with the law and outbursts of anger. I couldn't hold a job for more than a month. My friends all but gave up on me. My father kept funding me, hoping against hope that I would come to my senses.

One night, after drinking for hours, I went to visit a friend, who lived in the suburbs. I took the bus, and not knowing Minneapolis well, I got stranded in a suburb. My aggravation and frustration over my life reached a boiling point. Very disoriented, I went to a pay-phone booth and called a friend from high school. She picked me up and was very concerned. I was ranting and raving, and she sympathized with me but didn't know what to do. We drove to her place, and I called my last lover in New York and went on and on about how awful my life was in Minnesota and how I couldn't hold a job, all because he had interfered by calling my father and telling him that I couldn't handle things there. I loved New York City; I hated Minnesota. I was good in publishing; I wasn't good in anything else. It had taken me years of hard-earned achievement to get the jobs I had before my lover had ruined it all.

He listened to me and then said tersely and emphatically, "I know why you can't hold a job. You can't hold a job because you are a raving alcoholic!" Then he slammed down the phone.

No one had ever said this to me in quite the same way before. I hadn't fallen out of love with him, and it disturbed me greatly that he saw me as an alcoholic. Who knows why the obvious came as such a revelation? The next day, with the help of another friend, I found myself sitting in a chair at the admissions desk of a treatment center. There wasn't a single question about alcoholism to which I did not answer yes. After I had recited a little of my recent history, the admissions person stared at me and said bluntly, "If you don't get help, you are going to die. Fast." Not only was I an alcoholic, but apparently I was at the end stage of alcoholism, a progressive disease.

Even that first day, having been admitted for outpatient treatment on a government "Heart Grant" for low-income people without insurance, I felt free leaving the treatment center. The impulse to drink lifted. I don't know what I would have done had the staff also told me that I had not one but two diseases, that the demon I had isolated had an evil twin, and that it would take another two years before someone called that demon by its name.

I truly thought that my problems would end when I left the treatment center and attended AA meetings on a regular basis. It all made such sense. I believed my counselor who told me that if I stopped drinking, my problems would go away. The alcoholism had created the turmoil in my life; all I needed to do was not to drink, one day at a time.

My older brother had quit on his own and remained sober. Everyone in my family was getting healthy.

I returned to New York, found work as a literary agent, and again attained a false sense of well-being from the esteem that my literary talents generated. I fell right back in with the same crowd of writers, artists, and wannabes, and before six months had elapsed, I drank again. This time, though, I knew that something lay behind my taking this drink, something that took hold of my nervous system and changed it. Before I fell off the wagon, I could feel the tension of mania, and I was conscious for the first time of the incredible power of that disease. When I walked into a bar and ordered the first wine that I had had in a year, the person sitting next to me watched me gulp it down and said, "Well, thank goodness, now you look normal. When you walked in, I thought you were going to go through the ceiling."

Once I started losing weight and began to hallucinate, seeing the streets of New York City as Van Gogh-like smears of color and shapes, I knew that I was in trouble. For some reason, I even knew what I would call the trouble this time. "I think that I may be manic-depressive," I told my therapist. By then I had started the bed-hopping that characterized my earlier breakdown.

I couldn't keep going; I could tell that my thoughts were no longer connecting. After a three-day binge, during which I lost fifteen pounds, I showed up at my office, but I was barely standing up. I had felt like fainting in the elevator. Anyone could have seen that I was very ill. I told my new employer that I would have to go to a hospital right then.

I left the office against her wishes. My boss honestly thought there was nothing really wrong with me. I looked fine to her. But I could hardly walk the two blocks to the hospital. My feet were like lead weights, and my eyes told the whole story. I've looked into the eyes of other people who are in manic states, and those eyes belong to someone or something else. The nurse ushered me into the office of two doctors, who saw the whole picture in a flash. "You'll have to detox," the doctors said. "And there's probably something else wrong."

I had never been so grateful in my life as I was to hear these words. I honestly think I would have collapsed had someone not finally noticed the real distress I was in. My physical strength had kept others from really seeing that I had had this disease for years, but the doctors could see that I was in great pain. They shot me full of something that put me to sleep, and I slept for more than a day. When I awoke, a doctor stood at the foot of my bed. "Does your mind ever race?" he asked. "You think I'm manic-depressive, don't you?" I answered. He smiled, and then he wrote out a prescription for a drug that would save my life, lithium, which deflates mania at its most extreme.

I rebounded fast and left the hospital before I was ready. My boss had fired me, but I accepted the severance check and stepped back out onto the streets of Manhattan. Worried about money, wondering how I would find yet another job, the mania hit again the moment I left the office— it had never really left. I hadn't filled the prescription yet, and I couldn't get to the doctor to whom I had been referred until after the long Memorial Day weekend.

I went back to the hotel where I lived and fell into despair. I called my ex-boss, the only person with whom I hadn't reconciled yet, and I set up a time to meet with him. I talked fast over coffee, and for the first time, he was sympathetic. The emotional bond between us remained strong. "Try to stay off the bottle," he said, when we parted. I laughed and promptly went to a bar to find solace and consolation for my miserable existence.

When someone is in a manic-depressive state, the highs and lows come so fast and so furiously that it's like being on a Ferris wheel. Although I belonged to a regular AA group, by then I was so caught up in my other illness that I would not have thought of attending it. I did talk to one friend from the group, who also had a dual diagnosis. "Don't tell them that you are manic-depressive," he said. "They'll think you're crazy."

Walking home from the bar that night, I was pulled by the arm by a young man whom I had seen around. I blacked out from the time he grabbed my arm to the moment when I came to in his apartment to find we were having sex. I pushed him off me and ran. He followed, and as he got closer, I turned around and said something crazy, my eyes glaring. He backed off. Mania, if nothing else, was a defense against hostile strangers.

In my room following the rape, I packed my bags and called home. My father said he'd arrange airfare for me the next day and that I should get to the airport and onto a plane without stopping for a drink in between. I didn't fight it this time. I knew that I wasn't well. My energy came in bursts. I left a will, thinking I might die from overexertion. I was so thin I could barely lift my bags. I had almost no money and no idea how I would get to the airport, but I was supposed to meet someone from Minnesota in town for the day and I hoped he would give me a lift. Although I didn't know this person well (he was a writer whose work I had agreed to represent), simply knowing that I would see someone from home helped to relax me. The stresses of New York by then were so extreme to me that I felt safer in the company of the many Minnesotans I knew who also traveled frequently between New York and Minneapolis.

This acquaintance met me the next day and didn't question my obviously frenzied state. He could tell that I was high-strung to the point of collapse and immediately agreed to let me share a cab to the airport with him.

I stepped off the plane smiling. I was reasonably sane, and I knew what I needed to keep sane from now on. Off booze, on lithium. With that combination, I couldn't lose.

One day at a time, with the help of a family that supported me financially and emotionally on my return, I regained my balance and I managed better than I had since my breakup with my New York live-in relationship. Even on lithium, though, the manic-depression persisted, and I have since experienced a couple of bouts of disruptive depression and one major manic episode. I've lost jobs because of it. Inevitably I slip when I go too far "up," and the last time that happened, I nearly died from drinking to medicate my other illness. Drinking one carafe of wine during that last episode led to a 4.0 blood level; this was due partly to the mania, but also because I returned to the last point of my alcoholic progression.

The triggers are usually the same: conflicts with men, reminders of my past, job problems, and financial stress. Only since the last manic episode—which lasted six months and included three bad alcoholic bouts before finally landing me in a hospital—have I finally reached an acceptance of my past and, with that acceptance, serenity. Something happened the last time that integrated the fragments of my past: A doctor assisted me in handling flashbacks brought on by posttraumatic shock. We brought together episodes in my life that I had never processed or that I had blacked out. I felt as though I'd awakened from a twenty-year nightmare.

With all of the pain I have known and the ups and downs in my life, I believe I have gained as much as I have lost. I know there is a Higher Power, because I feel that only a miracle would have relieved me of the anger and self-destructive bitterness I had harbored for years. Only a miracle would have placed in my path people who extended their hands to me though there was nothing in it for them; these people helped me out when I appeared to them to be in distress, even though I couldn't give them much back, either financially or emotionally.

I feel better about myself than I have since I was eighteen, when I set out to conquer the world, eager and cocky, believing that I had something that no one else did. Humility is a quality that I cherish, peace of mind the most significant achievement I can imagine. When my father died five years ago, I kept going.

I know myself, a starting point that I couldn't reach until I had pushed both my demons back into the darkness from which they came.

Forgiving others and understanding the stigma and lack of information about manic-depression have been easier for me than for some other people I know. Nearly everyone in my life who has mattered, whether at work or in social relationships, has learned to put my diseases in perspective. They no longer take care of me, but they also don't blame me, and they help me to move on from episodes if they do occur. I, in turn, take responsibility for attending to a chronic medical illness and encouraging the spiritual balance that will keep me from taking a drink.

All in all, I feel lucky. Grateful to be alive—which no one who has not been near death can fully understand—I am renewed in my commitment to make the most of life. I have much less control over the manic-depression than the alcohol in the long run, but I no longer fear hospitalization when it is needed. I can breathe in and breathe out and feel free. This freedom includes the ability to love, something I had thought was lost to me forever.

Judy's Story

I WAS A PRETTY TYPICAL youngster, loved a lot, spoiled a little, and playfully scorned by loving relatives who found me too intense for my years. My mother, a nurse who hadn't worked outside the home since I was born, had tried most of those years to have a second child. Finally, when I was in the third grade, she had my brother, a blond, smiling infant who goo-gooed noisily most of the time. My father was a cop, handsome and cheerful in his scratchy wool uniform.

We lived in a big, dirty East Coast city where grass and trees were the exclusive possessions of the park. My mother, who firmly believed that children needed to be exposed to "green stuff" daily, would meet me there each day after school. I'd run from the school to one of the shady paths where I knew I'd find her pushing my brother in the old-fashioned baby carriage. I was in the fourth grade then, and I delighted in this afternoon ritual, its time for sharing, and maybe a cookie or two.

But one particular fall day there were no cookies, no hugs, no stories about spilled milk or gold stars on lessons. I could see that my mother had been crying, and I asked what had happened. Desperate and confused, she blurted out that my father, who had recently experienced some back problems, had just been diagnosed with bone cancer. I asked if that was bad. She told me it meant my father was dying. I remember my mind racing, my heart beating, my stomach feeling sick. I had never experienced panic, but what took over my emotions was surely panic, and it wouldn't let me believe her. I thought of the other options that we could still explore: more doctors, more nurses, medicines, surgery. Then I considered the supernatural avenues: Masses offered by priests, prayers by the nuns to the saints and the Blessed Virgin. All these would still have to be explored.

And they were explored, but to no avail. My father worsened, and what had been soft moans in the night rapidly became agonizing screams of pain. I made it through this awfulness because of my faith, which told me something that the others didn't know: God would make my father well again for Christmas, well enough to buy the electric train that my brother had seen in the department store window, well enough to sit on the floor with my brother and play with him on Christmas morning.

My father died on December 16; he was forty-one. I was eleven, and I had lost my best friend and God in one night. My father's death and my ensuing loneliness taught me many lessons. One of the earliest was the importance of praying with sincerity; another was the realization that happiness was impermanent.

My mother decided to move our lamed family to a small community in Kentucky, near her sister. Loneliness for the nurturing aunts and uncles I'd grown up with was overwhelming at times. During those years, I remember becoming easily distraught by the tragedies of the world—starving children, war, poverty—too easily, too often. Reading and my studies seemed to take my mind off such issues, and they soon became my most trustworthy companions.

After a bright high school career, I began studies at the University of Kentucky in Lexington, where I found that honors and awards required little emotional investment and offered great pleasure. I was one of the few women at the notorious party school who had come to study, rather than find a husband, but at the end of my junior year, a husband found me. While home on spring break, I met my brother's scoutmaster. Bob's Irish good looks, maturity, and easy laugh seemed the perfect prescription for a "little girl lost."

By our second year of marriage, Megan and Bob III had been born. I was busy and happy. Cooking, keeping up with two young ones, refinishing furniture, and transfers caused by Bob's job filled most of my twenties. Right after my twenty-ninth birthday, we were transferred from San Francisco to Kansas City (where we still live), but I became terribly homesick for the city by the bay, its museums, concerts, and cosmopolitan lifestyle. I blamed my less stimulating life for the depression and emptiness I could feel settling in on me. I have since learned, though, that the onset of major depressive illness typically occurs in the late twenties.

With the children in school full-time, I joined the PTA and a bridge group to occupy my time, but I never felt totally accepted. When serious bouts of colitis and debilitating headaches began, my internist ordered a minor tranquilizer. It quickly threw me into even deeper depression. Soon, what had been an unsure shyness had blossomed into antisociability, which in turn became isolation.

One autumn a few years later, I enrolled in a full load of difficult courses at the university, hoping to quickly finish an undergraduate degree. An eight-year absence from studies and the effects of the tranquilizers left me with little aptitude for scholarship. I was terrified that I had lost the ability to study and learn, which had long been a source of comfort to me. I pushed myself through several weeks of the semester even though panic attacks forced me into taking more Librium, and insomnia or nightmares filled most of my nights.

While driving to class one day, a fog of fear and anxiety overcame me. I could see the white rock wall that surrounded the campus, and I could feel the car moving toward it. I can remember wanting to merge with those rocks, to become as strong as they were. I felt my hands turning the steering wheel toward the wall, but as I went over the curb, I jammed on the brakes. I know that I wasn't injured, but I can't remember if any damage was done to the car. I do recall that as the car came to a standstill, I became suddenly aware that I needed more help than I was getting.

I drove to a local hospital. Doctors and nurses gave me some kind words, more tranquilizers, and a private overnight room complete with my own duty nurse who urged me to pray more—poor advice for a woman who still regarded prayer as an exercise in ritualistic futility.

Emotionally beaten, I withdrew from all classes and retreated to the safety of home, where my emotional health continued to deteriorate. The holidays came and went, but I remember little about them besides the fact that I learned my brother had become addicted to drugs. The previous year, we had been thrilled to find that he had been assigned to Germany, escaping duty in Vietnam. How shocked we were to realize that western Europe may have been far from the fighting, but its drug traffic made Vietnam's look paltry. This news drove me deeper into depression.

Bob eventually had to force me to leave our bedroom, where I had virtually imprisoned myself—shades pulled, no light, little food—for the drive to a private psychiatric hospital in my mother's hometown in Kentucky. In poor physical health and considerably underweight, I was unable to take most of the medications traditionally prescribed for my condition. With them, my hypotension caused me to faint frequently; without them, anxiety prevented me from engaging in either private or group talk therapy.

After six weeks of unsuccessful attempts to "fix" this situation, doctors advised Bob and my mother that electroconvulsive treatment was probably the only alternative to long-term institutionalization for me.

I didn't argue—I couldn't. Off medication, my mind spun constantly, jumping from fears for world peace to obsessive-compulsive religious worries. I could feel myself spiraling downward into greater and greater hopelessness. I would have tried anything that offered relief. Shock therapy gave me that relief. My treatments were humanely performed under anesthesia; they caused few unpleasant symptoms, and from the onset, they began to have positive effects. Soon, I was able to talk with therapists and in groups. Since my need for sedatives decreased, I was able to begin tricyclic antidepressants, which gradually restored my emotional balance and let me see light at the end of the tunnel. In April I was transferred to a Kansas City hospital for a few weeks, then finally released in May. Provocative treatment, prescription medication, and a lot of love allowed me to make an amazing recovery from the mental illness that I had feared would end my life.

Feeling as if I were back on track, I decided to take my therapist's advice: seek a challenging job and the beginning of a career. In the fall I began work in a large ad agency as a copywriter, and I loved it. Promotions, salary increases, and fulfillment came quickly after that, but Bob was less fortunate. He had been transferred again, but this time without us. In his new assignment, he lived and traveled out of Chicago for a year or so, returning home only on weekends. I waited and watched as the job took its toll.

Having buried both his mother and father from early deaths related to alcoholism, Bob had always rejected heavy drinking. But now, lonely for family and friends, he spent most of his nights in bars, and he carried a fifth with him in his luggage. Dulled by hangovers, desensitized by his responsibilities, and continually homesick, Bob was soon dismissed. His drinking only increased after his termination, and more drinking led to more failure, which led to subsequent job losses. I worked harder and harder to make the money he no longer did, but this only drove him deeper into a loss of self-esteem that kept him from enjoying any of my successes or those of the kids, who were now active high schoolers.

Bob's job losses—nine in ten years—a surprise financial slowing of my company, and growing personal problems haunted our marriage. No longer comforted by booze, Bob used violence to boost his ego. My face became familiar in the hospital emergency rooms; my emotional pain seemed unbearable. Desperate, I started drinking at night to curb anxiety and get some sleep.

My fall was rapid. Unlike Bob, a big man whose drinking career seemed still in its prime, my female physiology began to crumble under the effects of nightly drunkenness. Since alcohol countered the effects of my medication, my depression returned; my weight climbed to almost 200 pounds, and I was frequently overwhelmed by mixed feelings of paranoia, anxiety, and fear. My work slipped miserably, although I prided myself on not drinking during the day.

Two phenomena hastened my collapse. My mother was taken terminally ill, and the sixty-year-old company I worked for, unable to weather the recessions of the times, gradually moved toward bankruptcy. Mother died in May, but the company I worked for didn't dissolve until August of the following year, a month after I had been sent a formal letter of termination, citing excessive absenteeism and inferior work as reasons for dismissal. Signed by the vice-president who had promoted me four years earlier, the letter was brought to me in a hospital, where I was being treated for alcoholic pneumonia. Even though I had been hospitalized three times in the previous six months for similar illnesses or for suicide attempts, I saw no connection between my physical and mental illnesses and my drinking.

I was released from the hospital on a Tuesday morning, and I was drunk that afternoon, never having returned home. No longer employed, I occupied myself with staying just sober enough to function. I could no longer sleep without drinking, and I'd awaken several times each night to drink a little more from the bottle I kept beside the bed. One morning I awoke to notice blood on the bed linens. I rushed to a mirror to see my face cut and bruised, and I called Bob at work for an explanation. (In the wake of my uncontrolled drinking, he had been practicing a type of controlled drinking that had allowed him to hold down a job for a while.) He told me that I had fallen in the middle of the night trying to get to the bathroom.

As I stared at the swollen and bloody face in the mirror, I was overcome. I knew I had to try something—something besides the brief high I continually drank for—something besides botched suicide attempts that sought help from people I had already shoved away from me.

My daughter had left AA literature around the house, some of which I'd read and considered fairly sound, though way too religious. I decided to take my chances with the "God folks"—at least until I could learn to drink socially. So around 10:30 that morning, even though all I really wanted was a drink, I reached for the Yellow Pages and dialed an AA group far from my home. To this day, that group does not have an answering service, but as coincidence would have it, an elderly man answered and told me that the next meeting was at noon.

I was able to stave off the urge to drink until half an hour before I left for the meeting, when I poured myself a skimpy scotch, the sole remains of a half-gallon I had opened only the previous day. I checked to see that I had another fifth in reserve, threw on some wrinkled white shorts, tried to cover my cut face with makeup, and left the house, glass in hand.

It was a sultry July morning with temperatures already near 100. I turned the car's air-conditioning on high and headed for the bank building in which the group met. I entered a small room. There were less than a dozen people, yet I had the feeling of being suffocated by a crowd. My heart raced and the pain in my side (which I was later to learn was from an enlarged liver) thrust itself down into my legs. Ted, an older man with a cane, came toward me, took my trembling hands, and motioned for three women to take me into a side room with them. There, they asked questions about my health and urged me to go to a nearby hospital, but I refused. When I left, I could tell they never expected to see me again.

I drove home trembling but resolved. Inside the house, I longingly thought of the unopened fifth, but I began my calls and found that I still had medical coverage for another month. I then called the hospital, only to learn that it had no beds available. After swallowing my pride, I confided in the unit clerk that I really doubted that I would ever again find the courage I had at that moment. She believed me, and she soon called back to say they'd take me, even if it meant putting a bed in the hall. I had put off calling Bob because I suspected he would again try to persuade me to adopt his "controlled-drinking" efforts, which had never worked for me. My call to him proved me correct—he thought hospitalization was unnecessary, and he convinced me to wait to make my final decision until he came home.

As soon as I agreed, panic swept over me, and I realized that despite the tremors I had been experiencing, a small degree of peace had been with me throughout my efforts that morning. Encouraged, yet knowing my courage would dissolve in the wake of full-blown detox, I grabbed the unopened fifth and started drinking.

I think it was then that I called my daughter and maybe my son, but my memories are fuzzy. Bob arrived home, determined to change my mind, but I had already packed. He must have recognized that an argument might shove me from my melancholy stubbornness into the drunken anger he had seen so much over the last year. I think he also sensed that I was on death's path. So, knowing that he was about to lose the best drinking buddy he had ever had, Bob acquiesced, kindly helped me into the car, handed me the scotch, and drove me to the hospital. At 4 P.M. I was wheeled into admissions, in the middle of the main lobby, wearing the dirty white shorts and clenching the fifth tightly between my legs. Around 4:30, I finished the bottle on the elevator to the eighth-floor treatment center. And so, on the twenty-third of July, eight years ago, I began the long trek to recovery from a dual diagnosis of alcoholism and major depressive illness.

Treatment was not what I had bargained for. Doctors coldly announced I had liver malfunction that would "probably" go away if I stayed dry. Psychiatrists refused to counsel me until my system cleared of alcohol and the medications reached a therapeutic level. Therapists insisted on probing into my life, past and present, telling me that I could never drink again. They warned me how easy recovery was inside a treatment center and told me that my four weeks there would be worthless if I didn't follow them with regular AA meetings: ninety meetings in ninety days. I had never planned to be that faithful to AA; I had seen it more as a crutch that would be useful for a week or two after hospitalization.

The "God" thing in AA scared me. I feared that I would be forced back into formal religion, which had disappointed me so much; forced to face the God who had not wanted to let my father live; forced into the ritual and guilt that had made up my early faith. I celebrated my forty-second birthday in the treatment center, and Bob came to visit me, half-drunk. Night after night, when he'd visit, I could smell alcohol on his breath, and, of course, the staff could also. They tried to prepare me for what it would be like to go home to a drinking spouse, and they asked me to consider separation. Bob retaliated with anger, affirming for me the fact that his controlled drinking was not working, that his earlier violence still remained.

It was then that I learned how to pray, in the midst of a treatment center, surrounded by atheists and agnostics, street addicts and hookers, blue-collar workers and college professors. I learned to pray for guidance, not "things." I would lie in bed and ask for the help I needed to make it through the morning or, on bad days, through the next hour. When I learned to let others know my weaknesses, I was able to talk with people again. The Friday night sobriety party on the unit, which I had scorned upon arrival, became something I found myself looking forward to, and as my alcohol levels decreased, much of the intensity of my depression lightened, and I was able to sleep through most nights. I began to sense the miracle that was happening.

I was released from treatment on August 20, feeling rocky but hopeful. On the way home, I went to a noon meeting of the same group I had attended twenty-nine days earlier. Ted and the three women barely recognized me but heartily welcomed me back. They urged me to return frequently and I did—nearly one hundred thirty times in the first ninety days. I faithfully attended the three noon meetings and the seven evening meetings that group had each week. But my craving to drink was so strong and my fears so unsettling, I had to find other AA halls that were open all day. These halls were convenient for the courts and the cops who would bring in the less violent drunks from the street. I would go and sit in the hall, watching some men play cards or some youngsters bat a Ping-Pong ball around. Sometimes I would surreptitiously stare at the court-ordered folks who were still drunk, knowing I was only a drink away from their agony, praying that I could stay a drink away for the rest of that day.

Bob, hoping to "make it easier for me at first," decided not to drink for a while after I returned home. I saw him go through detox on his own that first week, but he would admit to no difficulty. He had joined Al-Anon, and its wise members urged him to come regularly, which he did. And then, after I had been sober about four months, one crisp fall morning, he walked into one of my morning AA meetings and sat down. When it came his turn to talk, he said simply, "I'm Bob, and I'm alcoholic." His twenty-year drinking career ended that quietly, and our sober life together began.

Today Bob and I are both active members of AA. Our daughter Megan, who has long been a vital part of the Adult Children of Alcoholics (ACOA) movement, left a career in retail several years back to work for the hospital I had gone to that July afternoon. She contacts insurance companies, seeking medical coverage for people who want to enter chemical dependency treatment. While insurance providers grow less willing each year to pay for in-hospital treatment, Megan doesn't weary of arguing for those who really want to change their lives. She has recently returned to school and is concentrating on studies involving the genetics and psychiatry of alcoholics.

Our son, Bob III, stayed pretty distant from the ACOA movement, not wanting to remember how much alcoholism had touched our family. After graduation, he married and took a job in marketing. Soon he had become a workaholic whose drinking frequently went beyond social limits. Bob and I talked frankly with him, but we sensed a denial about his own drinking that was similar to his views on our past alcoholism. Relying on our Higher Powers in such cases, we turned young Bob's problems over to those competent hands. Imagine our surprise when a year ago, still drinking regularly, he announced that he had accepted a position marketing the chemical dependency and psychiatric programs of the same hospital that employed his sister. And only a few weeks ago, he told me that he no longer enjoys nights out with the fellows when the purpose of the evening is to "get wasted." I guess there really are no coincidences.

I have truly been part and parcel of family recovery, but recovery must also be singular—just for oneself.

Seven years ago, I resumed my undergraduate work, twenty-three years after I had left school to marry, and I graduated with honors two years later. A year and a half ago, I completed my master's degree. Now I teach at the university from which I fled in suicidal frenzy almost twenty years ago. I can look out my office window and see the white rock wall—it's really quite beautiful, but I no longer want to become a part of it.

My gratitude has not diminished in my eight years of sobriety. Despite bankruptcy, boggling work and study loads, and the arguments and emotional traumas that accompany two adults sobering up in the same home, my gratitude level runs high. When I can take time from the task of earning a living, I revel in writing. I have much to share with those who are trying to climb out of the depths of dual diagnosis and onto the paths of recovery. I try to touch them and make their road a little less rocky, less steep.

It is in this spirit that I tell my story.

KATE'S STORY

FROM THE TIME I became aware of my beginnings (about the age of five) until I was eleven, life was a chase-and-capture game: a series of physical abuse and intermittent molestation. Despite all the evidence of abuse, I couldn't account for why I couldn't sit still or why I hyperventilated, heard voices, and had periods of time that I couldn't remember anything about. This went on and on. Even though I complained of the "lost time" now and then, nobody in a position of authority would listen to me. (I didn't hear anyone say it, but I expect the words "active imagination" were used here.) Those six years were simply hell on Earth; I thought nothing would be worse than being young and helpless.

The summer of my eleventh year, I began taking a mild tranquilizer. Though I did calm down a bit, I just didn't feel like myself, so one day I flushed the tablets down the toilet. I never mentioned that I wasn't taking them anymore, and my parents didn't seem to notice. Life continued with many hyperactive mishaps, and then I went off to college. Eventually my whole world turned upside down.

I didn't adapt well to college life at first. I shunned the people and the study halls and the parties, and mainly stayed to myself, reading science fiction books. In the beginning, I had no real friends, but I was eager to belong somewhere. I wanted to be alone, yet I wanted to belong, a contradiction that would spark many crises in my life. In college it sparked the most dangerous crisis of them all: a suicide attempt.

My first friend was Cindy, a big-city girl who liked to smoke, drink, and hitchhike. Up until now, I had done none of those things. She initiated me. I smoked cigarettes and drank with the wildest of them. I hitchhiked to small towns nearby and made out with men I didn't know. Sometimes I'd even smoke a little marijuana if someone happened to have some. I was quite a wild child.

But there was a clock ticking within me. I always felt I had very little time to live. And then one night everything fell in.

I was lying on my bed reading, when the lost-time syndrome came over me. I had been neither drinking nor doing drugs, but the feeling was the same, and suddenly the lights went out. When I woke up, I was on my back strapped to a bed in a hospital room. My parents were called. The deans of the school were notified. Drug testing was done.

Apparently I'd had some sort of fit, and my roommate had called the police. Everyone, they said, was scared to death. I had no memory of the incident, and except for feeling a bit tired, I was okay.

Nevertheless, tests were run, from EEGs to X rays, and I went home after a week with a bottle of minor tranquilizers. The diagnosis was chronic anxiety with psychomotor dysfunction.

After recuperating, I returned to college. Soon I was back to my old tricks with Cindy. Only this time, things never went as planned. I had blackouts while drinking and even became suicidal at times. Encouraged by my friends to take chances, that year I began mixing more and more of my tranquilizers with alcohol. At times, I would see two, three, four, and even five of everything. The game got more and more serious.

By my sophomore year of college, I was thoroughly depressed. I had stuck with Cindy and her friends, but they weren't the sort you talked to about personal troubles. So, listening to the voices in my head one day, I stopped at a drugstore and asked for a bottle of over-the-counter sleeping pills. Combining them with about eighty tranquilizers, I swallowed them.

I don't know what I'd expected to feel. I'd thought I would feel sad and maybe a little bit angry. All I felt was full. I lay down for my last sleep and gave no thoughts to anything in the world.

The sound of the school counselor's voice woke me. Through a kaleidoscope of colors, I saw her holding up two pill bottles. I heard her say, "If you'd really taken all of these, you'd be in the hospital on a slab."

Then I passed out.

The next morning, I miraculously awoke at 6 A.M., in the same clothes I'd worn through the night. I struggled from class to class. Cindy was a great help. When I told her how I'd tried to kill myself, she mimed holding a gun to her head. "Next time, just shoot yourself," she said.

My troubles with alcohol continued. I was much more careful about my medication but combining it, sometimes with twelve bottles of beer, was dangerous. I never knew how I'd react. But I seemed driven—by feelings I couldn't explain to anyone—to destroy myself little by little.

My parents were divorced by the time I finished school, so I lived with my mother for a while. To her dismay, I continued to drink and run around with none-too-acceptable friends. I openly smoked pot in front of my younger sisters, and often took off driving in the small hours of the morning, hell-bent on destruction. I thought I was doing just great: I had a job, a car, a stereo—what more could a young person want?

Eventually, inevitably, the roof fell in. Again.

I had purchased a brand-new bike. It was a beauty, a high-quality twelve-speed. I got it home and took it out for a spin. I got only halfway down the block before I noticed the chain was rubbing on the derailleur. I was reluctant to mess with a new bike, yet driven to distraction by this flaw, I got out my dad's old tools.

For one hour I sweated over the chain, and it refused to move. Then a feeling came over me—an overwhelmingly destructive feeling—and I began smashing and ripping at the bike with my bare hands. I didn't quit until even the frame was bent. Then I went into the house and told my mother I needed help.

For the next five years, I bounced in and out of detox centers, treatment centers, and psychiatric wards. I overdosed more than twenty times. I went through three different counselors. By the time I turned twenty-six, the helping professionals considered me not just a high risk but downright hopeless. Even I felt this to be true. Down on the bottom, crawling from rock to rock, I prayed a simple prayer: *Please, God, help me to want to live.*

For a long time, no answers came. Then a miracle happened, a psychotherapist named Etta. She had been recommended by a counselor in a treatment facility who said she was the best.

Reluctantly, I went to see Etta. And then I saw her again. And again and again. We talked at first about my past—I had much to talk about—and then we moved on to the present. Why did I think I was so self-destructive? I didn't know. Was it in my past? Partly. What about the rest of my behavior? I really, really didn't know.

Etta convinced me to see a psychiatrist. I was scared witless. He prescribed some non-mood-altering medications, and I promised to take them. But I hated the way they made me feel. I told Etta so, and she said to just keep taking them. I still worried about the past, so much so that I told Etta about my fears. She said, "I won't let anything like that ever happen to you again." Just like that. I could relax because I was in good hands.

But I didn't relax. I fought and fought. I cried and yelled at Etta and threatened to commit suicide. When that didn't work, I threatened to start drinking again. When even that didn't work, I gave up. I had finally met someone a hell of a lot stronger than I was, and I was strangely, deeply happy.

Then one day Etta quietly suggested that I was "predisposed." "Predisposed?" I asked. "What's that supposed to mean?" But then, much more came clear to me. The lost time meant periods of dissociating. The self-destructive, out-of-control episodes and the voices I heard happened during periods of psychosis. My wanting to be alone was an antisocial tendency.

To cut through the jargon, I asked Etta just what was wrong with me. Softly, she said that I had borderline personality disorder.

I was blown away for months, alternately crying and yelling until I thought even Etta's saintly patience would be worn thin. I pounded on blankets and pillows, and even on myself when I felt particularly angry. I thought the feeling of helplessness would never leave me, but it did. Only the progress was so slow, so painstaking, that if I had the option now, I think I'd rather die by suffocation than relive that period of my life. But I did pass through it. And on the other side, I found a solid but sad realization: Mental illness is forever.

I continued to see Etta and, with her encouragement, attended AA meetings. I was timid at first, and once again felt like an outsider, but I got to know a few people and felt better as time went on. The only thing that really bothered me about AA was that whenever I brought up my psychotic episodes, everyone tried to get me to talk about something else. They wanted me to stick to AA. I argued that AA was for *all* of me, not just the drinking part. Arguments broke out; one man yelled at me. Even my sponsor said, "I just don't understand being proud of yourself for merely taking a shower and eating dinner."

Pandemonium had been loosed, and I was at fault. My solution? Leave AA.

I talked with Etta at length about my experience in AA, and she said it wasn't uncommon for people with a mental illness to have trouble with other AA members. I wanted to know why. Etta said it was simple: absolutely anyone can wind up mentally ill, and I was a constant reminder of that fact.

So now I'm abstinent and trying to live by the AA principles and slogans. I apply them to my mental illness as well as my drinking problem. I find that the saying "This too shall pass" helps me tremendously during my psychotic episodes, and Step Two is invaluable when I feel self-destructive.

I also keep an open mind as far as AA goes and hope that some day I will have the courage to rejoin my friends. If I could wear a sign that said, "I'm mentally ill. Be gentle with me," I would. For, with the help of the Twelve Steps, I've learned a way of living with a mental illness that I couldn't have acquired through therapy alone. Whereas before, when I was drinking, I would wake up dreading the day and feeling like I should end my life, I now have energy and the bad times don't seem so bad anymore. As one man told me, "I used to have problems, but now I only have 'troubles.'" Troubles, I can handle; it's the self-loathing combined with an out-of-control feeling that I don't need anymore. There's a special joy in overcoming a psychotic episode without alcohol.

Since the day in my twenty-sixth year when I got down on my knees to say a prayer, my life has turned around completely. Etta has moved to another state, but I haven't forgotten about her. I remember all the hard times we had in therapy, and I smile to think that I was once considered hopeless. I'd like to give that hope back now. Even in my narrow wanderings I've met people with mental illnesses and alcoholism, and I've heard their stories of pain, confusion, and longing. Just like me, they deserve a chance too.

KATHY'S STORY

I WOULDN'T HAVE bothered to get sober if I hadn't gotten some relief from my depression. When I did get help, I felt like I was crawling out from under a wet woolen blanket and into a new world. I've managed to stay relatively free by continually working on my recovery, but recovery depends on treating both my depression and my alcoholism.

AA simply cannot do everything for me. I have to take antidepressants: I have an imbalance in my brain chemistry. Some people take insulin, I take antidepressants. I've had to learn to accept that I truly need them and that there is no shame in this. I've stopped listening to the comments of people who don't understand that antidepressants are not uppers; rather, they restore me to the starting position that people who haven't battled depression take for granted. I still have the daily struggle everyone has, but now I sleep through the night, I have an appetite at meal times, mornings aren't agony, I don't leave the room ashamed that I've started to cry again, and I no longer wish I were dead.

I come from a family of twelve. There was a high level of stress in my family. Depression, manic-depression, and alcoholism can be traced back several generations. Both my parents suffered from untreated depression; neither of them had self-esteem to pass to their children. Marital infidelity and compulsive gambling also hit my family hard.

John, my oldest brother, attempted suicide by overdosing on pills and alcohol when he was eighteen years old. He was narrowly saved. Rick, one year my senior, went into treatment at twenty-four because of his addiction to drugs and alcohol. Doctors told him that his liver was barely functioning, that in another few weeks he would have died. Thomas, one year younger than I, sold drugs. Michael, two years my junior, became ill at fifteen with manic-depression but was undiagnosed for several years.

Amid all this unhappiness and chaos, I developed expert caretaking skills. I stepped forward as the family hero, getting good grades, babysitting, cooking, doing housework, trying to make my mom happy and avoid making my dad angry. I developed the skill of minimizing. Compared to all the other family troubles, my moodiness seemed minor. In fact, I felt I was untouched by it all; I thought I had it together. I left home to go to college and eventually became a teacher. I wanted to change lives. I was concentrating all my energy on other people instead of myself.

I didn't start drinking until I was eighteen years old. I thought that if I was careful, I could avoid what my brothers had gone through. Still, I plainly remember the feeling of relief I got from my first drunk. I felt like I had found something I'd been missing all my life. I drank to take care of my feelings. I drank to shed loneliness. I drank for courage and then to quiet anxiety and guilt. I drank to sleep. I drank myself into strangers' beds. I made money decisions according to the cost of a six-pack. I drank every day. Later, when I moved to a new city by myself, I drank alone.

One summer, one of the most important people in my life was diagnosed with terminal breast cancer. She had been a professor, a mentor, and a friend. I was devastated. I wanted to stop everything and just be with her. She wouldn't allow it. She told me it could be many years yet and that I was to go on with my life. So, with no jobs to be had locally, I left the state that winter, determined to be as brave as she was.

I worked as a substitute teacher during the day and worked in a bookstore at night. The one person I did know in my new hometown promptly became engaged and moved out of state to be married.

One year later, I was twenty-six years old and a teacher. I fell into a relationship with a man who was thirty-four and a short-order cook. I agreed to live with him, thinking I would save money on rent. He became emotionally and sexually abusive; physical violence shadowed our interactions. Our relationship started with alcohol, and it continued with a steady stream of booze. His thirteen-year-old son moved in with us (a son I hadn't even known existed until about a month before he moved in). I was left to care for this nearly six-foot-tall boy, while his father worked nights and would come home drunk or high.

The relationship went from bad to worse. My lover lied to me and manipulated me. I, so blunted by alcohol and un-happiness, was unable to change course. I continued in the relationship, opening my checkbook over and over again, taking care of his expenses and neglecting my own.

He sent his son back to live with his ex-wife and decided he wanted to go back and finish his degree. An ex-Marine, he told me he was entitled to a GI loan, so I paid most of his tuition and living expenses, expecting to be repaid when the loan came through.

What I didn't know was that he had been dishonorably discharged and, in fact, owed the government money. There would be no GI loan.

When I began fearing for my safety, I slowly started to realize that I had to get out; with the help of a friend, I carefully began to make plans. I told my lover that at the end of the school year, I was going to spend the summer with my family. So he talked about finding another apartment. I rented a storage space and started packing up my things, taking a load over after work when possible. I blamed myself for our problems, and I think I convinced him he'd be better off without me. I'm sure his ego told him he would easily find another meal ticket.

I was lucky. I did get away from him.

That fall I went back to teaching. I found a studio apartment and tried to start over. The only thing that kept me going was denial. I felt helpless about my friend suffering from cancer, and I couldn't deal with the shame I felt about the relationship I had just left. I avoided the few people I did know. All I wanted to do was stay home and watch TV and drink.

I lost weight. In the shower, my hair came out in handfuls. The dark circles under my eyes reflected the fact I couldn't get to sleep at night and couldn't wake up in the morning. What sleep I got was punctuated by violent nightmares and leg cramps.

At work, my short temper turned into angry outbursts; sometimes I'd yell so loudly that my voice would crack and I'd need to hang on to a chair to hide the shaking of my hands. Instead of *saving* any of my students, I was becoming an abuser. (I felt as if I were watching my parents try to control our family of too many kids.) I hated my job, and I hated myself more. I couldn't keep up at work or dig out from underneath the clutter in my apartment. I was ashamed of my "laziness," my inability to even clean up my apartment. The guilt and frustration were overwhelming.

Inside my head was a growing pressure. I used to wish it would just be crushed. Often I felt I couldn't stand it. It seemed only drinking and television helped reduce the anxiety and craziness that built up inside me. I couldn't make decisions; my concentration was bad. My driving worsened. When I drove through yellow lights, I felt I was daring other cars to hit me. Still my denial was strong: *I* was not someone who committed suicide! I was just stressed out and not coping well with my friend's cancer.

To maintain my teaching license, I had to take a human relations class. The instructor, Mildred, had worked with cancer patients and their families, but she'd also worked with individuals on stress management and assertiveness skills. I was resentful that I even had to take the class, but I now believe it was no accident. I had no idea that Mildred would be instrumental in saving my life. In November I began seeing her outside of class for help in stress management. I still had no idea of the extent of my own problems.

I never gave myself enough of a break to even consider that I might be ill. I blamed hormones, PMS, stress, homesickness, and broken relationships. I thought I was just weak and disorganized. I never felt up and energetic. So I tried harder and harder to get my life together. I would get on the phone and call my sisters long-distance to help me get through another day. In one conversation, I asked Mary, "Don't you feel like I do?" I thought everyone felt life was simply to be endured.

She said, "No. I don't. Everyone gets down once in a while, but you're always down. It's not normal. Something is wrong with you." Her comment hit a deep chord, and I started questioning myself. (I can see now that my depressive episodes started in eighth grade, if not earlier.)

That winter I had told my mother I wasn't feeling right. She encouraged me to see a doctor. An appointment was made for two months later; I braced myself for the wait. My denial kept me from looking at my behavior. I felt as if I were losing strength in my hands, and at the same time, I thought there was something wrong with my car's steering wheel. On the way to work, my car seemed to fly around the curves of the interstate, barely under control. By early March, I decided to stop drinking for a while, since alcohol seemed to have no effect. Everything was flat.

On a Monday night in March, I had an appointment with Mildred, who asked how I was doing. I told her I wasn't feeling very well. She looked straight at me and said, "You're not telling anyone how you're really feeling. No one knows just how badly you do feel, do they?"

I started to sob. The big secret was out. I felt that she must know how bad it really was. She asked me if I thought I might hurt myself. I kept crying.

In a small voice, I said, "I just want some help. I can't stand this anymore. I just can't stand it anymore."

She offered to drive me to the hospital. I told her I couldn't go, I wasn't ready, I couldn't leave work, I had an appointment in April, and my mother thought I should go to a special clinic. Mildred told me she knew of a good hospital right in town and that I could get admitted before April. She told me I had a right to make my own decision.

I decided not to wait. It was the first time in my life I'd made a decision just for me.

That night I couldn't stop crying and I couldn't sleep. At 6 A.M., I called my boss and told him I wasn't coming in.

I cried all day, unable to get out of bed. The hospital called: The doctor had said it would be good for me to come in as soon as there was a bed. Later the nurse called and told me a bed would be available Thursday. It was now Tuesday. I couldn't believe all this was happening. Why couldn't I just snap back? I had spent my whole life trying to be good, and now everything was falling apart without my consent.

I went to work Wednesday and made arrangements for a substitute. I only told the people it was crucial to tell. After work, I drove over to a friend's. She drove me in my car to my apartment to pack some clothes. The world was moving in slow motion, yet inside me were panic and desperation. I didn't want any of this to be happening, but I couldn't stop it. Thursday night I was admitted into the hospital.

I felt I was the ultimate failure. I had no control over myself or my life—here I was, checking into a psychiatric unit of a hospital. By this time, my vision was dimming the lights and distorting the shapes of the rooms. Even *I* was moving in slow motion. I couldn't stop sighing. Whoever I thought I was, was receding down a dark narrow tunnel; nothing seemed to matter anymore.

The estimated ten days of inpatient treatment stretched into thirty days, with another month of outpatient treatment and three months of disability leave from my job. I thought I might never work again.

The hospital days were filled with therapy, learning, and healing. Getting to know the other patients with similar struggles was very helpful, too.

While an inpatient, I asked for an assessment of my alcohol use. After years of wondering, I decided to see what the experts had to say. I didn't like the answer. They said that not only was I supposed to deal with my depression, but

I was also supposed to give up what I felt was my only true friend, booze. I don't know how long I lay on my bed and sobbed that day.

I remember saying to my nurse, "I don't think I really have a problem with alcohol. My problem is just depression. I drank to medicate my depression." She replied, "Your problem is denial."

Still, I figured I had many more good drunks in me. I was only twenty-eight years old, and I'd had some great times drinking. A CD counselor, Bonnie, helped me. Bonnie was old enough to be my mother, with a kindness and generosity I couldn't get enough of. "I didn't think I hurt anyone," she said. "I successfully ran our household. I just quietly got drunk every night for twenty years. You're lucky you're facing this now. I wish I had those years back."

I knew I could easily drink away twenty years. I certainly had the heartache. Now the question was, *Did I have the heart to start a new life? Where would I find the strength?*

Eventually I found the strength in recognizing that I was winning a tough battle. The program at the hospital was intensive, and I had to be an active participant in my recovery. I felt I was being asked to change everything I knew in my life, with no idea of how it would all turn out.

All I knew was that my life had to change and that I had to trust that things would improve. And slowly I saw and felt myself getting better—it was all the proof of a miracle I needed. I was finding hope again after more than ten years of feeling none. I made friends with some of the patients, dear friends I still have. I learned that I could reach out for help and someone would be there. I was born into a new existence. If, as they say, happiness is directly proportional to how grateful one is, I am happy. I have gained a faith in myself I never had.

Still, I have thoughts of suicide occasionally, especially when I am feeling stressed or down. Ironically, it helped to hear that I will probably have these thoughts all my life. It is like my attachment to alcohol—I still think about drinking from time to time. I believe it is more than the fact that the diseases I have are "cunning" and "baffling." I believe that my mind has chosen alcohol and suicide as coping mechanisms, and so, as it sorts through options on how to deal with something, those two "remedies" come forward. Fortunately, I now see them as thoughts racing past—like a fast-scrolling message across a computer screen. I can read them, but I don't have to act on them. I have choices. I reserve the right to choose them at a later date, but right now, this day, I don't have to. I can't prevent thoughts from arising in my brain, but I don't have to let them command my behavior. I can watch them flicker across the screen in my head.

My recovery is ongoing, and I need company along the way. Being in the program has helped me to think differently about life and to change my behavior. Going out to an AA meeting each week helps me pare down the isolation I was so deeply enclosed in from the years of my illness. I've developed a bond with the people in my AA group that has let me see the importance of the commitment I've made to myself. I don't want to let myself down.

I am five years sober now—which is far longer than any romantic relationship I've been able to maintain. I see my psychiatrist to monitor my medications. I see Mildred on a regular basis because I am still learning from her. I keep a journal and write poetry. I stay in contact with friends who are working through their own mental health issues. I have started graduate school and am looking into a career change. Day by day, I am finding contentment in my life.

RAVEN'S STORY

I AM AN ALCOHOLIC and a schizophrenic, and I have dealt with this dual diagnosis for the past twelve years. What follows is the story of how I came to be diagnosed with a mental illness and, later, to accept my alcoholism and start on the road to recovery.

My childhood was happy, and I did well in school. In my senior year of high school, I was elected student body president. As a result of this and other activities, I was awarded scholarships to attend a private college in Los Angeles. While I had experimented with drugs in high school, the freedom from my parents at college led me to a partying lifestyle in which I smoked marijuana, dropped acid, took downers for fun, and took uppers to stay up late and study. I also drank a lot. Despite all this, I graduated with a B average.

My childhood dream was to become a lawyer. I was admitted to law school in San Francisco, but my drug and alcohol use began to take its toll. Halfway through that first year, I got very drunk one night and, while walking home, became violent. The San Francisco police took me to a psychiatric hospital and placed me in restraints. This was the first time I found myself in a psychiatric hospital; it would not be the last.

Needless to say, my grades were mostly F's for that first year of law school. In order to continue, I would have had to repeat most of my classes. At that point in my life, to continue would have been a waste of money.

I returned to Portland and went to work as a laborer for a construction company. When I got off work, I would hang out in the park, drinking cheap wine and beer with street people before going home to my roach-infested apartment. After showing up at work several times drunk or with a hangover, the company let me go. When I quit paying rent on my apartment, I was evicted. I was drinking up all my money.

I packed my backpack and took to the streets, selling my blood for money. I hitchhiked to Seattle, where I was arrested for assault during a blackout. I returned to Portland, checked into a cheap hotel, and decided I needed to go back to work. I landed a job at a nice hotel as a prep cook. I continued to drink and to smoke my drug of choice, marijuana. Six months into my new job, I had a psychotic break, brought on by my continuous intoxication. Once again, I wound up in a psychiatric hospital after hearing voices and thinking I was going to commit suicide.

My psychiatrist—whom I trusted, since I was desperate and had nowhere else to turn—first prescribed Thorazine and later haloperidol. He told me I suffered from a chemical imbalance that could be corrected with medication. I was extremely paranoid, and the medication did seem to help.

For four years, I was stable and able to work at a minimum-wage job for the hotel. But then I had another psychotic break.

I believed I was going to kill myself and this time take some people with me. Back to the hospital. This time I was put on something different: a time-release injection of Prolixin, which I got every three weeks. Again I was stabilized. I continued to drink and smoke pot, however, against my doctor's advice.

It wasn't until four years later that I went to an AA meeting and began to realize how powerful the denial of my drug and alcohol addiction really was. The things I heard at AA meetings really made me want to quit using, but I could not. Something would always happen. I would quit going to meetings on a regular basis and, soon thereafter, relapse. I tried Antabuse, but even that didn't stop me from drinking; it just made it less enjoyable. Besides, I could still smoke pot.

Finally, I quit my job at the hotel and traveled north, taking a job at a resort in a national park. There I picked up a DUI and another arrest for vandalism while in a blackout.

Once again I wound up in the psychiatric wing of a hospital, this time for only a week. Since my private psychiatrist would no longer see me (I didn't have insurance), I went on welfare, went to live in a group home, and got into treatment.

Finally, three and a half months ago, I gave up pot and alcohol for good—at least so far—one day at a time. You might say that I got sick and tired of being sick and tired.

I hope that one day I won't need an antipsychotic injection like I do now, but there was a time when I believed the diagnosis my doctor gave would stick to me for life. Today I think of myself as a recovering alcoholic who needs to take medicine for a mental illness.

I am back in school, studying to be a paralegal; last term I earned straight A's. I am in a semi-independent living situation and hope to be driving again by the end of the year.

ROBERTA'S STORY

I'M LEAVING OUT a great deal because I don't remember a lot and what I do remember either causes me great pain or is something I am unable to interpret.

My father, the survivor of a wartime prison camp, was a heavy drinker. My mother was both alcoholic and schizophrenic. Her insanity, schizophrenic communication, and bizarre behavior confused me so much that I didn't know what was really going on, let alone what to make of it. There was a great deal of abuse, mostly emotional but partly physical.

I married and quickly had three children. I was divorced before I was twenty and had lost my children in a custody fight by twenty-two. The severe depression I had at the time precludes specific memories of that struggle. What I can remember is that I had been on Valium, by prescription, since I was seventeen, and that my alcoholic drinking began during the custody fight. I've almost completely lost my memory of the time between losing the children and meeting and marrying my second husband when I was twenty-five. What I do recall is having a series of jobs that didn't work out and a series of unsuccessful relationships that I ended in a rage, as I had ended my first marriage.

The first Twelve Step meeting I went to was for Al-Anon, and it was because my mother and second husband were "the problem." I didn't stay with Al-Anon, I didn't "get" the program, and my husband and mother continued to be the problem for me, even though I drank too. Two years later, I made it into AA, but only because of my husband. He was forced into treatment by his employer, and he simply refused to go to treatment without me. So I went to my first treatment center codependently, and I didn't drink for about six months. Then my mother died, and I drank again. After all, I reasoned, I'm not the alcoholic, my husband is. After I'd been drinking for less than a month, I started doing some street drugs too, reds and pot. After about two more weeks, I ran away from home in anger.

I always kept a suitcase with a few clothes in my car trunk in case my husband got drunk and abusive. To that I added my valuables, a coat, and some necessities and took off. I was drunk and loaded on weed as I headed our brand-new car toward Los Angeles. A thermos of coffee, a bottle of scotch, and half-baggie of weed were on the front seat beside me. I indulged in them freely as I drove. Since I didn't make it all the way to L.A. that night, I took an expensive hotel room, but I don't remember where.

A friend of mine had a brother who lived in the L.A. area; I called him from the hotel. I'd thought that somehow this guy would be the love of my life, and I'd planned some kind of seduction, but I also remember having one of those famous moments of truth. When I did reach the brother on the phone, I told him I needed help. He came to my hotel, took me to his home, and then escorted me to AA meetings every night for a week—as it turned out, he was a recovering member.

But in the space of a week, without booze and weed, I went to pieces. From moment to moment, I couldn't remember where I was. I always wore sunglasses because without them I couldn't look at people; I was paranoid and thought every person I saw was looking at me. My memories of those AA meetings is sketchy at best; it was one of the times when I couldn't concentrate on what was going on.

The same sort of problem came up at home. One time I stood in the bathroom, confused about whether to brush my teeth, wash my face, or brush my hair: There were three choices, all at once, and there was no sequence I could follow. It was too much for me. I just stood there and cried and felt ashamed. I soon felt lower than a snake's belly; whatever I was doing wasn't working, and I was full of self-loathing. My friend's brother, realizing I was in trouble beyond anything he could help with, checked me into a hospital. I was exhausted from lack of sleep and trying to manage the terrors of the last seven days.

I realize now that if you plotted on a graph how crazy I was, the line would go off the paper. I only remember fragments of certain events of that period. I can't say how we got to the hospital or what I did other than go to AA meetings during that week. My memory of my time in the hospital is just as limited. But I do know that before I left the hospital's program—against medical advice—I was feeling better. I stayed sober that time for three and a half years in AA.

During the first several months of my new period of sobriety, my second marriage broke up, so the only stability I had was my sobriety and my job. Looking back, I think I avoided drinking and drugging during those three-plus years because I used every other cross-addiction. I shopped, ate, traveled, changed relationships and apartments, and so on.

The year I turned thirty-two, my father was hospitalized with cancer. The day he died, I drank and smoked pot to oblivion. I was off and running again.

I inherited a large amount of money from him and began spending it on any and everything my heart desired. It worried me that I couldn't seem to stop spending or drinking. I tried to get sober again by attending AA meetings, but I couldn't. I knew I needed help, so I sought an outpatient alcohol treatment program. I went to one group. In the middle of the session, I was asked to leave the group and to see a psychologist. I saw a psychologist several times about my depressions and was then referred to a psychiatrist for medication assessment. The psychiatrist said that I had cyclothymia, a mood disorder like manic-depression but with less severe periods of depression and hypomania. I was started on lithium carbonate.

I know now that I was asked to leave the group because I was talking nonstop; I was manic. Of course, I didn't tell the doctor that my mood swings were severe—I had lived with them for years, believing that the depression was a punishment for my misbehavior during the manic periods. I was ashamed and reported watered-down, rationalized versions of myself and my reality. I didn't want to report the truth—that I was a bad, damaged person (which I sometimes believed); I think I was afraid of being thrown into the "loony bin."

Less than three months after starting lithium, I was having fine hand tremors, I couldn't control my bladder, I had gained fifteen pounds, and I tasted metal in my mouth all the time. I complained to the doctor, and he sent me to have my lithium level checked. I thought he wasn't listening to me, so I stopped taking the lithium and stopped seeing the doctor and the psychologist. I severed my connection with AA and got involved in a new relationship.

Even compared to my usual relationships, it was an incredibly intense and stormy one. During that time, I spent the rest of my inheritance, one hundred eighty thousand dollars. Looking back, I can see that I was having the mood swings but that I wasn't aware of my disorder at that time.

The man I was involved with couldn't make a commitment to me. When he tried to tell me why, I was deeply offended. I saw myself as capable of anything, in touch with the spiritual in a special way, beautiful and highly intelligent. I couldn't understand what he was saying, how he could do this, or how he could leave me.

Being unable to let go, *I* decided to leave—a last-ditch ploy to bring him back. When it didn't work, I called my ex-husband and asked him if I could come and live with him. I felt I couldn't survive alone. I was still drinking, but he helped me anyway. I moved into his place, where we occupied separate rooms. While I tried to put our relationship back together, I was still pining over, hearing from, and seeing the boyfriend I'd just left in California. The emotional gnashing of teeth, the cuss-and-discuss with both my ex-husband and boyfriend, were torture for me. I escaped, generally, into the scotch bottle; I escaped from the house by attending school.

At the end of the semester, in December, I attended a party set up at a local bar by a woman I had studied with. I met a man there, and by the end of the evening, we'd gotten close. By February of the following year, we were married, and I had moved from my ex-husband's house to my new husband's house by the time of the wedding.

Over the next several months, I became depressed and sought help. I thought I was still grieving for the relationship in California. I was put on an antidepressant. I continued to drink. After a while, I felt better, so I stopped taking the antidepressant and seeing the psychologist.

Life went on. I got a good job working as a legal secretary. Within two months, I had quit in anger and irritation and had decided to try sobriety again. I remembered that my life had been better and that I had kept a job when I'd been sober before. I had to look for that better life again. I went back to AA, and in the process found Adult Children of Alcoholics (ACOA).

I went to ACOA as well as AA for about six months, and I found an ACOA therapist. After several more months, I decided I wasn't an alcoholic, I was just an ACOA, and so I drank again. I was told not to come to therapy anymore unless I stayed sober for six months, so I didn't go back. I just got drunker and sicker, until I knew I was drinking more than I'd ever drunk before and got scared. I voluntarily went into treatment at a women's treatment center. I remained sober for about eleven months, then I started drinking again. I was still married, and by this time, my husband had learned a little about recognizing alcoholism, so I spent more and more time, including nights, away from the house with someone who would drink along with me.

Eventually I quit my latest job in anger and agitation. My friend's drinking increased, and so did mine. We both got angrier and started arguing and having terrible fights. I went home and angrily, defiantly, drank there. I worked part-time temporary jobs now and again as I could. I don't remember what my mood was because I spent most of my time drunk.

I then discovered I was pregnant. The next day, my doctor told me I needed emergency surgery, that my pregnancy was tubal. Thus began a depression unlike anything I had ever known. There was nothing I wanted in this life more than to have another child. After surgery, there would be no hope left for me to become pregnant. I was thirty-nine years old, and I would never have the baby I so longed for. I stopped caring if I lived or died.

I had been depressed before, but this was different. I had always worked on talking myself out of depression, believing it was punishment for my bad behavior. This time there was no relief, and I didn't care. If I stayed in bed for weeks, it didn't matter, because I wanted to die. I would drink myself to sleep, with the help of the pain pills I got after surgery. Day and night, the depression continued. I'd cry when I woke up, because I was still alive and would rather have died in my sleep. I didn't want to go on. I drank glasses full of straight whiskey, washing down the pain pills. Within five weeks, I was huddled on the floor in a corner of my kitchen, screaming out in pain and horror; my husband was on the phone arranging to get me into another treatment center.

It was there, in the alcohol treatment program, that I was diagnosed as a manic-depressive. I was put on Tegretol, an alternative treatment used for those who can't take lithium. The unit was on the fourth floor, and its lecture hall overlooked the hospital parking lot. Patients would look out over the lot when it was time for visiting hours, watching for families and friends. I had looked only once since starting treatment.

But on the day the staff gave me my first doses of Tegretol, something subtle and powerful happened. When I went to the lecture hall, could actually see our car driving into the lot, and could see my husband get out and start toward the door, I had my first realization in thirty-nine years about my manic-depression and its effects on my life. It startled the hell out of me. Until then, I had been swept along in the storm, bobbing up and down like a buoy loosed from its mooring in an endlessly restless sea. Suddenly, it seemed so simple, now that I could concentrate long enough. Now I could do more than just *register* that there were cars and people in a parking lot. I could *feel* that it was our car and in it was my husband, and I knew that he was coming to see *me.* The joy that feeling gave me surpassed anything I had known for a long time.

After almost a year of sobriety, I became manic. I had been taking my Tegretol incorrectly and, as I have a history of doing, I'd stopped taking my antidepressant without telling my doctor. The result? I drove from California through Canada to Alaska in four days, fought with the girl-friend I was traveling with, flew back from Ketchikan, and then took two separate driving trips to and from California to see my children and attend astrological workshops. I charged clothes and hotels and meals and whatever I wanted, and I didn't think twice about how we'd pay the bills. The thought that should have come between the im-pulse and the action was gone. Before I drove back home the last time, my mood crashed, and I barely made it home be-cause of the depression. When my therapist and doctor sug-gested that I needed to go to the hospital, I agreed.

I have done much better since then, staying sober for more than sixteen months. It hasn't been easy, because now I have feelings to deal with—real ones. I don't know how to deal with feelings; before, I had always done something to escape them. It was especially hard for a while after it fi-nally hit me that I'm manic-depressive and that my life is riddled with lost dreams, holes, and torn places. When I fully realized the effects of my bipolar disorder, my alcoholism, and my posttraumatic stress disorder (from growing up with an alcoholic schizophrenic), I grieved deeply for many months. But I have made progress and remained sober.

Now, instead of acting completely on impulse, I can think first, something I've never been able to do before. And I can listen to my own thoughts; they no longer run too fast to hear. Sometimes I don't like being level; I miss the highs. But I don't miss the intense irritability and rage that often accompanied the highs and made me quit jobs and leave relationships. When I think I'd like to be manic again, I remind myself of what it was really like . . . when the party was over and I was alone and depressed. Today I don't have to spin out of control, I don't get lost in the car, I don't dread the morning after because of hangovers or depression, and I don't go on wild shopping sprees. I don't wake up in strange places, with strange people, or have to park my car on the side of the road until I'm able to drive again. I'm free from manic-depression driving me into relapse after relapse.

Right now, I think I'm between dreams. The delusional dreams of my illness are behind me in most ways, and my new ones are very tentative. When I remember how many of my old dreams died, I wonder if I can make these new ones into realities. But I have a different kind of faith to sustain me now. Before, I had the glittering faith of the manic; today my faith is firmer, grounded in reality.

Scott's Story

I CAME FROM a well-to-do family and was trained from early childhood to grow up and become a professional person of some sort. Everything seemed to indicate I would succeed in this endeavor as the years passed. I got excellent grades in school and was an excellent athlete. I did all the right things.

Somewhere around the age of seventeen or eighteen, I noticed that I wasn't feeling quite right mentally. Things were confusing, not making any sense, and I started losing my sense of connectedness. To deal with this, I started drinking alcohol more and more. I was very lonely and unhappy. My parents and others tried to help me "snap out of it," but to no avail.

The year I entered college, I developed a serious drinking problem and, as I learned later, crossed over the line from social drinking to alcoholism. Maybe I'd crossed over earlier; I don't know. Let me tell you, being arrested for drunk driving several times and spending time in jail was not fun.

©Schizophrenics Anonymous, c/o Mental Health Association in Michigan.

Anyway, I got sober by entering treatment and Alcoholics Anonymous about a year later. I was exhilarated, although things still didn't seem to be quite right. I felt lost. About fourteen months into my new life, I decided to (once again) find some meaning in my existence. While on a trip with an acquaintance, I noticed things were really quite different. The leaves in the wind seemed to be talking to me. Cloud formations had special meanings. Television and radio shows were talking about my life. I thought I could read people's minds and communicate with them without speaking. I thought I had found the state that great spiritual leaders termed "being spiritual." I truly believed I had been blessed by God and that I had a direct pipeline to Him. I felt happy and scared at the same time. I was in a different world.

About one week later, I decided to travel out to the West Coast to really find myself, given my newfound power. While traveling, it seemed as if God's voice entered into my thoughts and told me that if I wanted real peace and power in my life, I should run my car off the road and leave the rest to Him. I did this, only to find no peace, rather a totaled car and a trip to the state mental hospital.

Since that time, I've been dealing with a disease called schizophrenia. It's been an uphill struggle. At the time of this writing, I believe I've found a way to pull myself out of a psychosis and to feel connected like I did before the alcoholism and schizophrenia. Today I feel at peace, own a thriving business, and have a wonderful relationship with my wife. We're in the process of planning a family.

This has been accomplished through the philosophy of Schizophrenics Anonymous, Alcoholics Anonymous, and a few special people in my life.

WILLIE'S STORY

BEING THE YOUNGEST in my family caused problems for me. I was always overprotected by my parents and older brothers. I was never given the opportunity to do things for myself; everything was done for me. That pampered treatment was not to my liking, and I rebelled at the age of twelve. I wanted to be my own man.

After graduating from grammar school to junior high, two of my closest friends and I decided that we should each get a bottle of alcohol. I got extremely drunk that night on a half-pint of mint-flavored gin, and I had to sneak into the house. That was my first drunk. Shortly after that experience, I had my first stick of reefer, along with some cough syrup. Soon I got comfortable with being under the influence, and at thirteen, I looked forward to my weekend allowance so I could buy alcohol and drugs. They made me feel terrific and, most of all, powerful.

I felt powerful in the sense that I was around other people and they couldn't detect what made me tick or what gave me the confidence I displayed at this young age. There weren't many kids into alcohol and drugs, so I felt special. The few kids I regarded as friends tried to persuade me to stop using. It wasn't long before I experienced a change: I abandoned all the positive things I had been taught by my parents, and I didn't allow myself to think about God or anything spiritual.

My personality changed so drastically that I flunked seventh grade. I had an I-don't-give-a-damn attitude because I was indulging in alcohol and drugs regularly. My parents were very upset. My mother knew something was wrong but couldn't figure out what it was. She took me to the principal and asked if I could be placed in my proper grade, because she knew I could do the work. The principal, too, felt that according to my grammar school grades, I shouldn't have failed. He gave me another chance, provided I made the honor role during the first marking period. I made the honor roll, and the principal kept his word. My parents were now monitoring my school work, so I did just enough to pass. During all this time, I continued to abuse alcohol and drugs. I graduated from junior high school to high school, only to be kicked out in my freshman year.

Out of school, I had a lot of time on my hands. I spent it in the pool hall and gambling joints, supporting my drug habit. I was now a poly-drug user who consumed any and every type of drug available: reefer, microdots, black mollies, THC, CIBAs, red devils, airplane glue, hashish, nutmeg spice, Valium, cocaine, heroin, pollutants, cough syrup with codeine, and, of course, alcohol. Eventually I found a drug of choice: heroin.

At seventeen, I became a father and at eighteen, a husband. Nonetheless, I continued to abuse drugs. At nineteen, I began hearing voices. This scared the hell out of me, but I continued to abuse drugs. Then suddenly one day, I sensed an international conspiracy against me. For three weeks,

I refused to eat or leave my bedroom; eventually my wife got me to a hospital.

I was committed to the state hospital for three months, where I continued to abuse drugs, drink alcohol, and smoke grass until I was discharged. Being diagnosed as a paranoid schizophrenic seemed to impel me to drink and take drugs more than ever. I didn't want to think that I had problems. After discharge, I found myself recalling some of my experiences in the hospital—attempted suicide, nearly choking to death when attendants strangled me with bed sheets, and being knocked out with drugs that were put in my food. Because of this treatment, the idea of conspiracy seemed all the more probable. I'd never trusted any psychiatrist or counselor. As a matter of fact, I loathed professional people, because whenever I dealt with them they pretended to be like God.

Although my mental health issues needed to be addressed, I continued to abuse alcohol and drugs. I compounded the problem by using street drugs on top of prescribed medications.

Shortly after being discharged from the hospital, I got a mediocre job. I lost it after four months for being intoxicated.

Over the years, I had a few, more productive jobs, but they never lasted for any length of time. I still hadn't seen the light or realized what those chemicals were doing to me. At the age of twenty-four, I found myself again at the state hospital: drinking, drugging, and being in denial about my mental illness. I spent three months in the hospital, and much of what had happened during my first stay happened during the second.

After discharge, I again chose to abuse alcohol and drugs. I'll omit listing the ways I supported my drug addiction over the years; the things I did aren't easy to think about or write about.

By the grace of God, my wife and our two sons and daughter were still with me. For years I raised hell with them. I was nothing but a burden to anyone who dealt with me.

After staying out of mental health hospitals for fifteen years, I was to return once more. Being hospitalized and thinking about doing away with my wife and kids finally made me hit bottom: It was time to leave alcohol and drugs alone. This happened in August seven years ago. I knew that Alcoholic Anonymous meetings were available on Friday nights, so I asked the doctor if I could attend. I was given outside privileges and went the two Fridays of my fourteen-day stay. Upon discharge, however, I went back to the same pattern of drugging, but this time, I knew I was getting tired—tired of being tired of everything. My wife encouraged me to keep going to AA, and every now and then, I did attend a meeting. Yet I continued to drink and drug and continued to be tired of the whole rotten scene.

Eventually I decided to put myself in the hospital to be detoxed, but while in the hospital, I had friends bring me alcohol. I also had access to drugs, but since drugs didn't do for me what they had in the past, I no longer abused them. I completed the alcohol and drug program and felt very good about it—I wasn't used to completing what I started. I also felt good about taking the initiative to get help for myself: I knew there had to be more to life than just a drink or a drug.

But even after completing the program, alcohol continued to be a problem. A year later, I went to an outpatient rehab. For the five months I was there, the staff members stressed going to Alcoholics Anonymous as an adjunct treatment.

I learned a lot about alcoholism, and although I was still drinking, AA began making sense to me. I started going to meetings three or four times a week.

I enrolled in adult education classes to get my GED. When I attended the classes, I was still drinking. The results from the GED exam showed that I had failed by one point. I reasoned that had I been sober during class, I probably would have passed. Two months later, I applied to take the exam again. I continued to go to AA meetings, and I didn't drink until classes were over.

Then one day when I was drunk and home by myself, tears started streaming down my face. It seemed as if my whole life were passing through my mind. I dropped to my knees and began to pray that God would deliver me from the obsession to drink. After the prayer, I passed out on the floor.

Days passed by without a drink. I continued to go to AA meetings and was encouraged to get an AA sponsor. I'll never forget asking an AA member to be my sponsor: he said he'd be honored, and I was elated. I made progress in overcoming my alcoholism and was eventually given responsibility for opening the facility for the AA meeting, making coffee, arranging chairs, and greeting people at the door. This went on for two years.

The second time I took the GED exam, I passed, which paved the way for enrollment at the community college. At that time, I had three months of sobriety. I now have six years of not using alcohol or street drugs. My life has changed from darkness to daylight. In getting sober, I experienced many obstacles, but I recognized them as part of the recovery process.

Throughout the years, I've been taking medication for my mental health problems, but I complicated my recovery by using mood-altering street drugs along with the prescribed psychotropic drugs (Thorazine, Stelazine, and Artane). The first group canceled out the second's beneficial results. Yet by the grace of God, today I'm healthy and sober.

I am very grateful for the opportunity to facilitate the STEMSS (Support Through Emotional and Mental Serenity and Sobriety) groups. They have given me self-esteem, purpose in life, and support.

I don't know where life will lead me, but I hope that I will never return to the damnation of alcohol and drugs. I am grateful to my Higher Power for guiding me to the doors of Alcoholics Anonymous.

Dual Recovery Anonymous

A blueprint for developing a Twelve Step program for men and women who experience both chemical dependency and an emotional or psychiatric illness

DUAL RECOVERY ANONYMOUS: A BLUEPRINT

Timothy H.

Introduction

THIS SECTION OFFERS suggestions for developing a recovery program for men and women who experience both chemical dependency and an emotional or psychiatric illness. The ideas, based on the Twelve Steps of Alcoholics Anonymous, are the result of extensive discussions with men and women in different stages of recovery from dual disorders, in different parts of the country, over the past several years.

Do People Who Experience Dual Disorders Need a Separate Twelve Step Program?

Yes, there are several reasons why a Twelve Step program is needed for recovery from dual disorders.

First, those of us who experience dual disorders are affected by social prejudice and by the stigma of mental illness. Prejudice and stigma are part of a larger social issue, but when negative attitudes and beliefs show up in a Twelve Step group, the results can be disastrous.

Second, many men and women who have been diagnosed with a dual disorder say that they have received misguided advice about their diagnosis and the use of medication at Twelve Step meetings. Some have been told that they do not have an emotional or psychiatric illness, and that they are experiencing merely self-pity or some other character defect *(You don't need those pills; they'll cause you more problems and If you're taking pills, then you're in relapse and not really sober).* Individuals who have followed such advice have experienced relapse: some have been hospitalized; some have returned to alcohol or drug use; some have attempted or even completed suicide.

Third, the existing Twelve Step programs were not developed to address the problems of dual disorders. They offer neither direction nor guidance for dual recovery *based on the personal experience of others.*

Fourth, existing Twelve Step programs are unable to offer the degree of emotional acceptance and support that is needed and deserved for people in dual recovery.

Some individuals are fortunate. They have been able to find a Twelve Step meeting that has some appreciation of emotional or psychiatric illness, and they cherish the support they get for their sobriety. Nevertheless, they may feel uncomfortable sharing their *dual* recovery needs openly and honestly. They may still find themselves feeling the need for secrecy in a program of honesty. Unfortunately, they may gradually minimize, deny, and ignore the other half of their recovery needs.

Fifth, the existing programs are single-purpose organizations—one disease, one recovery. Dual recovery does not fall within their primary goals. People who have a dual illness recognize that it cannot be divided into simple and separate parts. They acknowledge that while they do find support for aspects of their illness from available groups, they also need a group in which they can look at their total illness and recovery needs.

At present few programs have been developed by people in dual recovery. Prejudice and stigma about mental illness continue to create problems for individuals in dual recovery, both inside and outside existing fellowships. It does not appear that dual recovery groups are likely to form as special-issue groups under the organizational structure of the existing Twelve Step fellowships. Therefore, an independent Twelve Step self-help program needs to be developed.

Moreover, a complementary program needs to be developed for the loved ones of those who experience dual disorders. Parents, spouses and significant others also need assistance as they begin to struggle with their own recoveries.

What Will a DRA Program Be Like?

The DRA program is based on three simple ideas, which are suggested as a foundation for dual recovery:

- Today, I will be free of alcohol and other intoxicating drugs.
- Today, I will follow a healthy plan to manage my emotional or psychiatric illness.
- Today, I will practice the Twelve Steps to the best of my ability.

Will DRA Differ from Other Twelve Step Programs?

In order for DRA to help people who are affected by dual disorders, the concepts of the Twelve Steps need to be extended in order to include the recovery needs of both chemical dependency and psychiatric illness. Here are some quotations from people who are beginning to work on their dual recovery.

Powerlessness

• The illness has developed; it has already happened; for me it is simply a fact.

• I cannot always predict when the urge to use and setbacks of psychiatric illness may occur, how long they will last, or how intense they will be.

• I am powerless over the events that have occurred during episodes of my illness.

• I am powerless over the fact that I need to make changes in my life to treat my dual illness if I want to be healthy and safe.

• I am powerless over the fact that some of my abilities, skills, and efficiency have been affected by my illness, some that I may not completely regain.

Unmanageability

• Because of my illness I have not been able to be the parent, spouse, provider, friend, and spiritual person that I have wanted to be.

• I have not managed to avoid a growing list of problems and consequences.

• I cannot manage to stop or control my illness on my own.

• I have not managed to hang on to my self-respect, confidence, hope, security, inner freedom, and vision of the future.

Higher Power

• I need time for my brain and body chemistry to rebalance; time to learn and practice the how-to's of dual recovery; time for my relationships to heal.

• Practicing the program of recovery with my Steps and medications is *Good Orderly Direction*; I know that even if I am having severe symptoms, which may include loss of contact with reality and memory loss, I know that my Higher Power will care for me.

• Appropriate medications help reduce my symptoms.

• I believe that a Higher Power has created the blueprints for the medicines we need and that researchers are gradually finding them.

• I have symptoms that come and go, but I am always okay on the inside. It's just my biological machinery that has the problems.

• I look for my Higher Power to give me what I need in order to cope with my illness: hope, faith, courage, wisdom, strength, and patience. What I look for in my Higher Power is care, not cure.

• Sometimes I am uncomfortable when I think of a "Higher Power." The concept brings up uncomfortable images, feelings, and memories, some of which are related to prior religious beliefs that are hard for me to separate from my family and early life experiences. Some of these concepts are tied to my using days, when I was into occult beliefs. For me, it is just too early in recovery to deal with this concept; it is overwhelming. What works for me instead is to think of a *Helping Power*—in other words, my direction, the paths I need to follow. Helping Power suggests the tools that I need to use and the time that I need to practice them.

Progression

In dual disorders, as in addiction, there seems to be a progression of common experiences. Individuals in dual recovery begin to find that they have shared many similar experiences, even though their particular illnesses may be different.

• First, a "no-fault" illness begins. It may have a sudden onset or develop slowly. Sometimes it seems to take on a pattern of its own.

• Second, the illness produces symptoms that are experienced in a variety of ways. They may affect one's thoughts, emotions, sensations, and perceptions.

• Third, the symptoms become disruptive and begin to interfere with one's ability to function, to relate to others, and even to relate to oneself.

• Fourth, the individual begins to experience problems and consequences as a result of his or her impaired skills and abilities.

• Fifth, the person attempts to protect his or her feelings, security, loved ones, and freedom. However, since the person's ability to cope is affected by the illness, he or she may begin to act in self-defeating or self-destructive ways.

• Sixth, the people who are close to the person with a dual disorder are also affected. They lack adequate information about the illness to clearly recognize the symptoms or know how to help the individual find appropriate help. Unfortunately, families then learn to cope with the illness in unhealthy ways.

Personal inventory

Directly and indirectly, a *personal inventory* is part of several Twelve Step programs. It is a process that helps people identify, relate to, and accept their illness. Inventories can also help people learn to monitor and manage their illness and to cope more effectively with setbacks and relapse.

Assets and liabilities are frequently the focus of an extensive inventory. This flexible category includes attitudes, behaviors, beliefs, coping methods, and memories:

• I need to have a clear picture of what I have that's working *for* me and working against me if I hope to have a chance at recovery.
• My greatest liability, "stinkin' thinkin'," includes my negative attitudes, beliefs, expectations, and assumptions. Stinkin' thinkin' leads me to stop practicing the Steps and go off my medications. This, in turn, allows my psychiatric symptoms to return and perhaps leads to a relapse to drinking or using drugs.
• Some of my liabilities have been with me since childhood, and others have developed over time as a result of my illness.
• Stress can cause my illness to become worse. Some of my stress liabilities are my ACOA and codependency issues, my anger and feelings of loss that are related to the grieving process about having developed a mental illness.
• I need to know the pattern of my illness if I am going to learn to live and cope with it. What are the warning signs? How can I recognize when I am becoming lost in the symptoms rather than coping with them?

Assets are the foundation of a dual recovery:

• My greatest asset is that after years of crises and illness, I learned to recognize and accept that I do have assets.
• Following a suicide attempt, I regained my willingness to survive and thrive. I experienced a challenge to live and create, and to be a part of something new.

• I believe that my interests, abilities, talents, and skills are assets.

• A major asset for me is that I care about myself, my family, and my friends, and that I can usually show it.

• I am stubborn in a positive way. I am determined to get the help that I need and deserve.

• My faith. The time of sobriety that I had before my mental illness happened.

Sanity and insanity

The Twelve Steps for dual recovery identify the need to be "restored to sanity." This concept applies to both chemical dependency and the psychiatric illness. It is looked at from two points of view: biological insanity and insane "stinking thinking."

Biological/physical insanity refers to changes in perception of reality as well as changes in the emotions, sensations, judgments, and behavior because of chemical or biological changes. These changes can occur as a result of psychiatric illness or from the use of alcohol or drugs.

Insane "stinking thinking" refers to attitudes, beliefs, expectations, and coping behaviors that are clearly self-defeating and self-destructive. Stinking thinking is frequently related to unhealthy defense mechanisms and to denial of the chemical dependency or psychiatric illness.

• My symptoms affect the way I think, my attention, my memory, my concentration, the way my body feels, my appetite and sleep, my behavior, and the way I relate to others.

• When I began to feel like myself again in the hospital, I felt like I was coming out of a serious blackout, but I had not been drinking or getting high.

• I went to work and sat at my desk. My mind simply would not work. Nothing made sense; I could not do the job I had been doing for a long time.

• A dual disorder is a strange illness that causes me two kinds of chemical insanity. My psychiatric illness changes my body chemistry, which can make me pretty insane, and my chemical dependency may trigger an urge to get high again, despite the problems and consequences I have already experienced. If I relapse into addictive illness, I get intoxicated and alter my thinking, feelings, and behavior. To recover from this insanity, I need to stop taking intoxicating chemicals and then I need to take appropriate prescription chemicals so I won't act insane.

Insane attitudes, beliefs, and coping

For many this is the same concept as stinking thinking, and many people believe that stinking thinking is a central part of the relapse process in chemical dependency. The same may be true of emotional or psychiatric illness. Here are a few points of view:

• I have had setbacks and relapses with my illness. When I have been working my program to the best of my ability and my symptoms recur, I see that as a setback. Perhaps my medications need adjusting or changing. Perhaps it was a strong cycle of the illness. But if I think I am doing so well that I decide to go off my medications, skip my doctors' appointments, keep my actions a secret, and believe I'm doing okay, that's pretty insane. And then when the symptoms recur, I don't see that as a setback, that's a relapse.

• When I feel symptoms starting and I go into denial about it, that's insane thinking.

• When I stop challenging the voices I hear.
• When I think that I can use alcohol to treat my symptoms.

What Problems Can Occur
In a DRA Group?

Two situations can create serious problems for a DRA group and can damage the credibility of DRA as a new Twelve Step program. (These concerns, however, are by no means unique to DRA or to the problems of dual disorders.)

The first situation arises when members of the group begin to offer advice on the diagnosis and treatment of emotional/psychiatric illness or chemical dependency. DRA is a nonprofessional self-help program based on the Twelve Steps. It does not offer treatment services (although some members may in fact be professionals in the fields of mental health or chemical dependency). Every individual at a meeting is there for his or her own dual recovery.

The second situation occurs when members get sidetracked onto issues other than the Twelve Steps and *personal* dual recovery. This is understandable, because many have not had the opportunity to speak with others in dual recovery, with others who take medication to treat emotional or psychiatric illness, or with others who have experienced frustration and resentment in receiving professional services. The problem occurs when the meeting comes to dwell on *problems* alone. "Problem-bashing" is counterproductive and creates barriers to solutions. Focusing on ways to cope with resentments, losses, and frustrations related to those issues will take the individual, and the group, further into recovery. (DRA, of course, has no opinion on outside issues.)

Each member in dual recovery has a valuable message to carry to others faced with a dual disorder. We carry the message of the Twelve Steps and the experience of our personal dual recovery. Slowly we learn to protect our opportunities and our ability to carry that message. We can build bridges of trust and mutual respect only by earning and maintaining trust with others. This is in keeping with the precept of attraction rather than promotion.

Should DRA Engage
In Public Education?

The purpose of DRA should remain twofold: personal recovery and carrying the message to others who are afflicted. The task for DRA is to develop our Service Center to help others who wish to start their own groups and to network with DRA as a whole. (See Resources listing for address.) To avoid any confusion of roles, education and advocacy need to be carried out apart from DRA by an independent organization. Therefore the Dual Recovery Network Association is currently being formed out of concern for people affected by those with dual disorders, their families, and their loved ones. (See Resources listing for address.)

DUAL RECOVERY ANONYMOUS: MEETING FORMAT

DUAL RECOVERY ANONYMOUS is a Twelve Step self-help program for individuals who experience both chemical dependency and an emotional or psychiatric illness. Men and women who currently use psychiatric medications under a doctor's care, or who have done so in the past, are welcome to participate.

OPENING
Welcome to the ————— meeting of Dual Recovery Anonymous. This meeting is open to DRA members and to other individuals who are concerned about their personal recovery. My name is————, and I am in dual recovery. Will you join me for a moment of silence, followed by the Serenity Prayer?

God grant me the serenity
To accept the things I cannot change,
The courage to change the things I can,
And the wisdom to know the difference.

Would anyone like to read the Preamble?

Preamble

DRA is an independent, nonprofit, self-help organization. Our goal is to help men and women who experience a dual illness: We are chemically dependent and we are also affected by an emotional or psychiatric illness. Both illnesses affect us in all areas of our lives: physically, psychologically, socially, and spiritually.

The primary purpose of DRA is to help one another achieve dual recovery, to prevent relapse, and to carry the message of recovery to others who experience dual disorders.

DRA has two requirements for membership: a desire to stop using alcohol and other intoxicating drugs, and a desire to manage our emotional or psychiatric illness in a healthy and constructive way.

DRA is a nonprofessional self-help program. There must always be a clear boundary separating the work of DRA from the work of chemical dependency and mental health professionals. The DRA fellowship has no opinion on matters of diagnosis, treatment, medication, or other issues related to the health-care professions.

The DRA fellowship is not affiliated with any other self-help organization or Twelve Step program. DRA has no opinion on the way other groups address the problems of dual disorders and dual recovery. We do not criticize the efforts of others.

The DRA Central Service Office will offer support to others who wish to start DRA meetings and who wish to work with other groups to carry the message.

Thank you.

ANNOUNCEMENTS
Are there any announcements at this time?

INTRODUCTIONS
Shall we take this time to introduce ourselves? Some of us are comfortable using the following introduction: My name is [first name, last initial] and I am in dual recovery. But there is no official introduction. Feel free to find a way of introducing yourself that you are comfortable with.
Would anyone like to read "Accepting Differences"?

Accepting Differences
Newcomers and visitors may ask, *Can a DRA program help me even with the type of symptoms that I have?* Such feelings are not uncommon. We need to help newcomers recognize that a variety of symptoms are possible with a dual illness. There is no single type of dual disorder.

Our chemical problems also vary. For example:

• One man used alcohol, while another used many different drugs.
• One woman got high daily, while another got high only once a month.
• Some of us have been in treatment programs several times for our chemical dependency, while others have received outpatient care while living at home.
• Some of us have been clean and sober for a long time, while others have yet to become abstinent.

We have found that this is also true when we consider the symptoms of our specific psychiatric illness and worry that they will set us apart from others. For example:

• Some of us use prescription medications to control our symptoms, while others have symptoms that need no medication.

[234]

• Some of us have struggled for many years with our psychiatric illness, while others have just begun to experience the onset of symptoms.

• Some of us have experienced changes in our ability to perceive reality clearly and have experienced hallucinations, whether they come in the form of hearing voices or seeing visions.

• Some of us have felt increased energy or have experienced changes in our ability to think and make judgments. We may have also found that our thoughts sometimes race and seem to go out of control.

• Some of us have felt a loss of energy, a loss of enjoyment of life, and have perceived life from a negative perspective. Perhaps our sleeping patterns and appetite have changed as well. We may have become suicidal. We may find that we have difficulties with our thoughts and concentration.

These lists are far from complete, but they point to a common bond: both men and women are affected by different types of no-fault illnesses whose symptoms can disrupt the ability to function and relate to others effectively.

Some of us feared that we were becoming hopelessly impaired. We came to believe that we would never be "normal" again. Many of us have experienced great shame and guilt. We believed that our emotional or psychiatric illness and chemical dependency were our fault. Some of us have become secretive. We tried to keep our drinking and drug use a secret, and later some of us felt a need to keep our recovery and Steps a secret. We also felt our psychiatric illness must be kept secret, especially if our recovery program included prescription medication.

We seemed to run out of ways to protect our feelings and self-esteem, and to protect ourselves from the attitudes of those around us. Many of us gradually went into a closet of denial. If there are any among us who have felt as though they were living in that closet, we welcome you. We want you to know that the fear, isolation, and secrecy no longer need be a part of your life.

Would someone like to read "Getting Started in Dual Recovery"?

Getting Started in Dual Recovery

The DRA approach to dual recovery is based on a simple set of ideas and Steps. They are suggestions for recovery rather than a set of rules. They encourage us to find our own personal recovery, the one that is most meaningful. They are meant to support those of us who wish to bring a spiritual dimension to our dual recovery.

The DRA program is worked on a day-by-day basis. Here are the suggestions for dual recovery:

- Today, I will be free of alcohol and other intoxicating drugs.
- Today, I will follow a healthy plan to manage my emotional or psychiatric illness.
- Today, I will practice the Twelve Steps:

1 We admitted we were powerless over our dual illness of chemical dependency and emotional or psychiatric illness—that our lives had become unmanageable.

2 Came to believe that a Higher Power of our understanding could restore us to sanity.

3 Made a decision to turn our will and our lives over to the care of our Higher Power, to help us to rebuild our lives in a positive and caring way.

4 Made a searching and fearless personal inventory of ourselves.

5 Admitted to our Higher Power, to ourselves, and to another human being, the exact nature of our liabilities and our assets.

6 Were entirely ready to have our Higher Power remove all our liabilities.

7 Humbly asked our Higher Power to remove these liabilities and to help us to strengthen our assets for recovery.

8 Made a list of all persons we had harmed and became willing to make amends to them all.

9 Made direct amends to such people wherever possible, except when to do so would injure them or others.

10 Continued to take personal inventory and when wrong promptly admitted it, while continuing to recognize our progress in dual recovery.

11 Sought through prayer and meditation to improve our conscious contact with our Higher Power, praying only for knowledge of our Higher Power's will for us and the power to carry that out.

12 Having had a spiritual awakening as a result of these Steps, we tried to carry this message to others who experience dual disorders and to practice these principles in all our affairs.*

ROUNDTABLE DISCUSSION

This is a closed meeting where we can discuss the Steps and matters of personal recovery. Everyone will have an opportunity to share as we go around the table. If you do not wish to share, simply say "Pass."

---

*Adapted from the Twelve Steps of Alcoholics Anonymous. The Twelve Steps of AA appear on page 241.

CLOSING

Tradition Seven reminds us that every DRA group is fully self-supporting. As we close, a basket will be passed. All donations are used for our literature and other group expenses.

Tradition Twelve reminds us of our need for anonymity. We ask that you do not repeat the names of anyone who has attended this meeting or talk about what has been shared. Only by exercising this tradition can DRA provide a setting where we can feel safe to share in a way that will help our dual recovery.

If you know someone who might find help from the DRA program, feel free to bring them to a DRA meeting. However, please bring them only if they express a personal interest. Recovery is always a matter of personal choice. We can do our best when we carry the message and practice the program.

Would all who care to join me in the "Serenity Prayer"?

God grant me the serenity
To accept the things I cannot change,
The courage to change the things I can,
And the wisdom to know the difference.

RESOURCES

Al-Anon Family Group
Headquarters, Inc.
P.O. Box 862, Midtown Station
New York, NY 10018-0862
(800) 344-2666

Alcoholics Anonymous
World Services, Inc.
468 Park Avenue South
P.O. Box 459
New York, NY 10163
(212) 870-3400

The Anxiety Disorder Association
of America (formerly The Phobia
Society of America)
6000 Executive Boulevard, Suite 513
Rockville, MD 20852-3801
(301) 231-9350

Depressive and Manic-Depressive
Association (DMDA)
222 South Riverside Plaza,
Suite 2812
Chicago, IL 60606
(312) 993-0066

Dual Recovery Anonymous
Central Service Office
P.O. Box 8107
Prairie Village, KS 66208
(913) 676-7226
*A self-help organization for those
with dual disorders (Twelve Step
format).*

Dual Recovery Anonymous – Canada
294 St. Vincent Street
Barrie, Ontario L4M 4A1
(705) 722-6443

Dual Recovery Network Association
P.O. Box 8107
Prairie Village, KS 66208
(913) 676-7226
*An advocacy and education service
program for those with dual
disorders.*

Emotional Health Anonymous
2420 San Gabriel Boulevard
Rosemead, CA 91770
(818) 240-3215
*A Twelve Step program for people
with psychiatric problems.*

Gamblers Anonymous
3255 Wilshire Boulevard, #610
Los Angeles, CA 90010
(213) 386-3789

GROW, Inc.
2403 West Springfield
Champaign, IL 61821
(217) 352-6989
*A self-help program for people with
psychiatric problems.*

Narcotics Anonymous
World Service Office
P.O. Box 9999
Van Nuys, CA 91409
(818) 780-3951

National Alliance for the Mentally Ill
2101 Wilson Boulevard, Suite 302
Arlington, VA 22201
(703) 524-7600
*Support groups for persons with mental
illness and their families.*

National Clearinghouse for Alcohol
and Drug Information
P.O. Box 2345
Rockville, MD 20857-2345
(301) 468-2600
(800) 729-6686 (800) SAY-NOTO

National Institute of Mental Health
95600 Fishers Lane
Rockville, MD 20857
(301) 443-4513

National Mental Health Association
1021 Prince Street
Alexandria, VA 22314
(703) 684-7722

National Mental Health
    Consumer's Association
311 South Juniper Street, Room 902
Philadelphia, PA 19107
(215) 735-2465
Support groups for the mentally ill.

Obsessive-Compulsive Foundation
P.O. Box 9573
New Haven, CT 06535
(203) 772-0565
*Support groups and newsletters for
people with obsessive-compulsive
disorder and their families.*

Overeaters Anonymous
P.O. Box 92870
Los Angeles, CA 90009
(213) 618-8835

Sex Addicts Anonymous
P.O. Box 3038
Minneapolis, MN 55403
(612) 399-0217

Sex and Love Addicts Anonymous
SLAA Augustine Fellowship
P.O. Box 119
New Town Branch
Boston, MA 02258
(617) 332-1845
*Twelve Step groups for sex and love
addicts.*

THE TWELVE STEPS OF *
ALCOHOLICS ANONYMOUS

1. We admitted we were powerless over alcohol—that our lives had become unmanageable.
2. Came to believe that a Power greater than ourselves could restore us to sanity.
3. Made a decision to turn our will and our lives over to the care of God *as we understood Him.*
4. Made a searching and fearless moral inventory of ourselves.
5. Admitted to God, to ourselves, and to another human being the exact nature of our wrongs.
6. Were entirely ready to have God remove all these defects of character.
7. Humbly asked Him to remove our shortcomings.
8. Made a list of all persons we had harmed, and became willing to make amends to them all.
9. Made direct amends to such people wherever possible, except when to do so would injure them or others.
10. Continued to take personal inventory and when we were wrong promptly admitted it.
11. Sought through prayer and meditation to improve our conscious contact with God *as we understood Him,* praying only for knowledge of His will for us and the power to carry that out.
12. Having had a spiritual awakening as the result of these steps, we tried to carry this message to alcoholics and to practice these principles in all our affairs.

---

*The Twelve Steps of AA are taken from *Alcoholics Anonymous,* 3d ed., published by AA World Services, Inc., New York, N.Y., 59-60. Reprinted with permission of AA World Services, Inc. (See editor's note on the copyright page.)